Teachers as Servant Leaders

Joe D. Nichols

ROWMAN & LITTLEFIELD PUBLISHERS, INC.
Lanham • New York • Toronto • Plymouth, UK

Published by Rowman & Littlefield Publishers, Inc.
A wholly owned subsidiary of The Rowman & Littlefield Publishing Group, Inc.
4501 Forbes Boulevard, Suite 200, Lanham, Maryland 20706
http://www.rowmaneducation.com

Estover Road, Plymouth PL6 7PY, United Kingdom

British Library Cataloguing in Publication Information Available

Library of Congress Cataloging-in-Publication Data

Nichols, Joe D., 1957-
    Teachers as servant leaders / Joe D. Nichols.
      p. cm.
    Includes bibliographical references and index.
    ISBN 978-1-4422-0452-2 (cloth : alk. paper) — ISBN 978-1-4422-0453-9 (pbk. : alk. paper) — ISBN 978-1-4422-0454-6 (electronic)
  1. Teachers—Professional relationships. 2. Educational leadership. I. Title.
    LB1775.N53 2011
    371.1—dc22

                                                                    2010025744

♾ ™ The paper used in this publication meets the minimum requirements of American National Standard for Information Sciences—Permanence of Paper for Printed Library Materials, ANSI/NISO Z39.48-1992.

Printed in the United States of America

To Get
Her love, support, and sustaining spirit remain as my constant inspiration.
She is a true servant leader.

And to Manna, Micah, and Bethany,
three wonderful kids who serve without knowing.

Leaders we admire do not place themselves at the center; they place others there. They do not seek the attention of people; they give it to others. They do not focus on satisfying their own aims and desires; they look for ways to respond to the needs and interests of their constituents. They are not self-centered; they concentrate on the constituent . . . Leaders serve a purpose and the people who have made it possible for them to lead. . . . In serving a purpose, leaders strengthen credibility by demonstrating that they are not in it for themselves; instead, they have the interests of the institution, department, or team and its constituents at heart. Being a servant may not be what many leaders had in mind when they chose to take responsibility for the vision and direction of their organization or team, but serving others is the most glorious and rewarding of all leadership tasks.

—J. Kouzes and B. Posner

Contents

~

Acknowledgments

I would like to acknowledge past and present faculty and students within the Oklahoma City Public Schools; Moore Public Schools in Moore, Oklahoma; Fort Wayne Community Schools in Fort Wayne, Indiana; and those in the School of Education at Indiana University-Purdue University, Fort Wayne, Indiana. Without knowing, their inspiration, feedback, support, friendship, and experiences over the years have helped to shape my life, and my approach and attitude toward learning, living, and service. In as much, my immediate family and close friends must also share the credit for anything I have accomplished, will accomplish, or have become.

Professionally, I would like to thank those who have reviewed different portions of this text and who have consistently provided ongoing constructive feedback and suggestions. To the staff, reviewers, and editors at Rowman & Littlefield, specifically acquisitions editor Patti Belcher and her editorial assistant, Jin Yu, I appreciate your support and your efforts to make this process a pleasant and worthwhile experience.

~

Introduction

In 1977, Robert Greenleaf published the book *Servant Leadership: A Journey into the Nature of Legitimate Power and Greatness*. In his collection of articles, he provided inspiring insights and developed the concept of servant leadership, with a specific focus on the perspective of business, the academic world, and from the perspective of politics and governmental organizations. In each case, he focused on the ability of each of these entities to encourage optimal performance by embracing the concept of servant leadership.

For Greenleaf, optimal performance in the business world was not necessarily measured in stock gains or sales revenue, and in the world of government and politics, it was not measured in running a strong election campaign or "controlling" constituents with the use of power and privilege. In terms of teaching and educational institutions, optimal performance was not measured with gains on standardized tests or reproducing memorized knowledge from students with a high degree of variance within their own backgrounds, personalities, and learning styles. He also suggested that the power of leadership and authority can often be misused in the case of coercive power, where domination and manipulation are the central goals. In contrast, it can also be used to create opportunity and alternatives that support and provide autonomy for those we serve.

Coercive power can be cruel, overt, brutal, and, at times, subtly manipulative, often resulting in strengthening resistance from the one who is being controlled. On the other hand, servant leaders are fully human, and they are "functionally superior" because they are closer to the ground, they hear things, see things, and know things, and their intuitive insight is exceptional (Greenleaf, 1977). Their ultimate goal is not to control or manipulate, but to create an environment that allows shared power and autonomy, one that centers on stewardship and service as an ultimate goal.

The premise of this book is to center the focus of servant leadership specifically on the teaching profession. If anyone has taught for an extensive amount of time, they know that effective teaching is one of society's most complex, challenging, and compelling endeavors. Good teaching requires that we progressively become better-educated teachers ourselves, as we grow in our understanding of our teaching fields, cultivate our abilities to communicate effectively, and enrich our understanding and effectiveness in guiding multiple social and intellectual interactions within the classroom and the educational environment (Simpson, Jackson, and Aycock, 2005). This challenge becomes even more intimidating when we suddenly realize that we need to be prepared to also help the public (which includes caregivers, community and business leaders, politicians, school board members, friends, and neighbors) to better understand the realities and challenges of the teaching profession.

People who understand the teaching profession in a true genuine sense realize that teaching is more than knowledge of subject matter, pedagogy, and perhaps the gifted ability to interact with others. It includes a set of understandings, activities, interactions, relationships, beliefs of families, children, communities, democracy, ethics, forms of inquiry, critical thinking, and creativity. The belief that teaching is an unproblematic, simple, and straightforward undertaking is a perpetuated myth that is a serious hindrance to both current and future teachers, and one that will fail to advance the teaching profession as a whole.

For many years, the educational profession has lost sight of or has been distracted from the notion of teachers as servants to their students, their students' families, the education profession and the school administration, and the local community. Teachers have been inundated with more state and federal standards, more assessment, more pressure to improve test scores, and more accountability. In some cases, teachers rightfully have been challenged to improve their teaching skills and to show that their students are becoming more engaged, active critical thinkers and learners. In our exuberance (either by our own desire or that of politicians) to advance these outcomes, we have also lost a sense of the need for service and stewardship and the opportunity to serve our educational community in a greater sense than simply improving test scores and graduation rates.

No one will argue that the teaching profession needs to prepare students for future jobs in a shrinking global world and higher education opportunities where skills like critical thinking and problem solving are essential. But we might also argue that this academic and cognitive preparation should also be coupled with creating and encouraging students to become decent and ethical individuals who also consider the needs of others within their community and who ultimately serve first and lead by their example of stewardship and commitment to others.

Therefore, as we encourage and promote servant leadership, who is the enemy? Who is the culprit that is responsible for mediocre performance? Who is standing in the way of a better educational system that is not defined by simple increases in test scores, but by the creation of more worthwhile and caring individuals that ultimately define a better future society? The real enemy, perhaps, is intelligent and vital educational leaders and their failure to lead with a servant-leader attitude. Too many settle for being critical "experts" who make excuses for poor teaching and thus poor student performance, and who are unable or unwilling to undertake the hard tasks of building better educational environments in an imperfect world. In the words of Robert Greenleaf, "[educational] leaders have too little disposition to see 'the problem' as residing in here and not out there. In short, the enemy is strong natural servants who have the potential to lead but do not lead, or who choose to follow a non servant. They suffer. Society suffers. And so it may be in the future" (Greenleaf, 1977, 45).

A firm note of hope exists, no matter how bleak our current educational and political structure may appear in its discouragement of servant leadership. Police officers, firefighters, and first responders continually serve their communities, despite the venture into the unknown and inherent dangers of their professions. Physicians continue to serve their patients, despite the long hours and time away from their family. Social workers continue to serve children and their families, despite poor compensation, heavy case loads, and the complications of working with social service providers and overburdened court systems. Teachers and educators continue to teach and serve children, despite increased demands from federal and state governments, larger class sizes, shrinking financial resources, and, at times, poor compensation and an overall lack of respect from the community. Despite these great challenges, servants continue to serve, understanding the profound reward of their labor.

This introduction and the chapters that follow are an attempt to offer hope for educators and for those they serve. The first several chapters define teaching, leadership, service, and stewardship through an educational lens, and then provide information concerning how teachers can be more effective servants to their students, parents, colleagues, administrators, and communities. Choosing service over self-interest and having the ability and desire to lead others toward this goal—despite challenge and adversity—is a difficult journey, but a noble cause that ultimately may effectively revolutionize our definition of teaching and service.

Teachers as Servant Leaders

CHAPTER ONE

~

The Teacher as Teacher

It is a surprising and memorable, as well as valuable experience, to be lost in the woods any time. Often in a snow storm, even by day, one will come out upon a well-known road, and yet find it impossible to tell which way leads to the village.

—Henry Thoreau

Early Descriptions

Teaching is certainly the noblest of professions, and at the same time, one of the most frustrating endeavors that one will ever undertake. Particularly in today's political environment, with the ever-increasing use of standards and federally mandated exams in the name of accountability, the teaching profession has ceased to be an art form of multidimensional issues that include pedagogy, creativity, and inquiry. If we are not careful, it will continue to become a profession that is focused on an exercise in a futile race toward creating a mindless generation of students who respond to an appropriate "correct" answer without the development of critical thinking skills and the reflective ability to be a part of the next generation of contributors to our ever-evolving and ever-shrinking world.

Thoreau's quote at the beginning of this chapter begins to suggest that the best and greatest learning and teaching experiences may occur as happenstance journeys through unforeseen snowstorms and less-traveled paths through the woods. Other educational theorists and philosophers agree in kind that exploring, examining, discovering, and wandering are all good things, despite the rigidity that we are accustomed to when we experience "formal" education. One of Thoreau's friends and mentors, Ralph Waldo Emerson, also noted similar sentiments in his journal *The Art of Discovery and Learning*, as he reflected on the adventure of two friends: "Now here are my wise young neighbors who instead of getting like workmen into a railroad-car where they have not even the activity of holding the reins, have got into a boat which they have built with their own hands, with sails, which they have contrived to serve as a tent, and gone up the river Merrimack to live by their wits on the fish of the stream and berries of the wood" (*Emerson in His Journals*, 223–24).

Both Emerson and Thoreau, as well as others, envisioned an education that does not simply pass on the end results of past cultural creations but immerses each student in the entire cycle of experiencing, formulating, and then reinstating these formulations back into experience to test, hone, and modify (Bickman, 1999, xix).

Thoreau's emphasis on lived experience as an essential and crucial element of education has been used repeatedly to justify entirely random and unstructured educational approaches where discipline and rigor are shunned, "book learning" is scorned, and the role of the educator is diminished to the point of demanding some form of evidence that, in fact, something has actually been learned (Kohn, 1999, viii). As dedicated as Thoreau was to freedom and practical, experiential learning opportunities, however, this freedom was not without some rigorous instructional and learning approaches that set the stage for the mind to embrace creativity and exploration. It has been said that Thoreau rewrote *Walden* seven times before he had it in a form that satisfied his sense of artistry, and worked with a steadfast discipline and purposeful intentionality on almost everything he did. The rumor is that the great American author Ernest Hemingway rewrote the ending to *Farewell to Arms* thirty-nine times before he was satisfied with his effort (Tichy, 1988, 24). The discipline to labor long and hard and to insist on the same kind of diligence from pupils is too often confused by the progressive suggestion that a child often learns "by doing." As Thoreau suggested in his own writing and life, children actually learn by exploration and by constructing new ideas, but also by reading, listening, writing, and rewriting until the combination of effort and hard work blend inconspicuously with creativity and exploration. The intricate mixture of a pedagogy that combines the will to combine exacting standards with rhapsodic and unstructured learning speaks volumes for the true nature of learning and teaching experiences.

Traditionally, teaching required intellectual competence, integrity, independence, and a spirit of scholarly inquiry. In a pure, *scientific* sense, teaching is the transmission of both theoretical and practical knowledge and includes the development of one's own personal skills and techniques to enhance this process, as well as encouraging the development of these traits and attributes in one's students. Our central mission, then, as teachers, according to this broad *scientific* definition, is to generate and disseminate knowledge and to have our students gain this knowledge using their abilities or those that they somehow acquire during their educational careers. But certainly, the art or pedagogy of good teaching is more than being just a dispenser of information and knowledge. Above all, the superior prerequisite for becoming a good teacher should include a great passion for teaching, encouraging, and working with students, and above all, the ability to stimulate student interest and enthusiasm.

Leaving the pure scientific definition aside, teaching is more than simply dispensing knowledge. It is more than having students regurgitate memorized facts and trivia. And it is more than creating a competitive educational environment where only a few students are motivated and made to feel capable and competent. As teachers, we are involved in the whole child on a daily basis and hold a significant portion of their well-being in our hands. As a young teacher, Haim Ginott came to the frightening conclusion that "I am the decisive element in the classroom. It is my personal approach that creates the climate. It is my daily mood that makes the weather. As a teacher I possess tremendous power to make a child's life miserable or joyous. I can be a tool of torture or an instrument of inspiration. I can humiliate or humor, hurt or heal. In all situations it is my response that decides whether a crisis will be escalated or de-escalated, a child humanized or de-humanized" (1972, 15).

The position of teacher holds great power and even greater responsibility. The implication of Ginott's quote is twofold: The teacher sets the environment for learning and affirmative interaction to take place, and the teacher has the potential to encourage the child to become a humanized and accepted individual within the classroom environment and within a community of learners. Good teaching requires the abandonment of the concept of teaching as a technocratic trade or mechanical process that requires minimal talent, preparation, and freedom. Too many individuals pursue the teaching profession simply as an alternative choice to another career, without any clear passion for students and their learning and development. We cannot hope to attract the next generation of highly talented teachers who enjoy the art and thinking of teaching unless we continue to attract a significant number of young teachers whose commitment to children and society over-rides the repugnance of the subculture of schooling that legislatures and policymakers allow to exist and, at times, help to create (Simpson, Jackson, and Aycock, 2005). This statement begins to suggest a need for pedagogical liberation. The progressive educational philosopher John Dewey once stated, "Since learning is something that the pupil has to do himself [herself] and for himself [herself], the initiative lies with the learner. The teacher is a guide and director; he [she] steers the boat, but the energy that propels it must come from those who are learning" (LW 8:140).

Pedagogical liberation, then, requires a freedom from specific constraints and standards where the true science and art of teaching can be nourished, implemented, and encouraged and where the teacher as navigator or helms-man becomes the guide, director, and steersman of learning and discovery. With this freedom, the stage becomes set for classrooms of students and teachers to navigate the waves and to steer themselves through snowstorms in the woods toward their own sense of learning and self-discovery.

Philosophical Perspectives

The purest definition of the word *philosophy* comes from the Greek words *philo* (love) and *sophos* (wisdom). Literally, philosophy means the love of wis-dom and knowledge. Although I have already quoted the likes of Thoreau, Emerson, and Dewey, most philosophers would agree that the study of broad concepts like wisdom, knowledge, courage, etc., has the impact of influenc-ing the decisions and course of our lives. Coming to grips with these global ideas and values and understanding how we interpret these issues from our own varied personal backgrounds and experiences sets the stage for our own internal and reflective growth.

Every civilization and country has had some way of educating its young people. When considering educational philosophy, or more specifically a philosophy of teaching and learning, you must consider what it means to be educated and what the process of "education" and "learning" should actually accomplish. Alfie Kohn, in his text *What Does It Mean to Be Well Educated?* (2004b), even suggests that instead of creating schools and classrooms and fitting children into a system of how we think they need to grow and learn, we consider working backward by starting with what we're looking for in terms of long-term objectives, and then asking ourselves what kinds of class-rooms and learning environments we need to construct. Once we conclude what kinds of classrooms we need, we should ask ourselves the question of what kind of teaching is most likely to produce the results we want, and more importantly, what kind of teaching is likely to get in the way of our goals and objectives.

Although this is not a specific text on the philosophy of education, it is important to review the general theories of education as they are of practical importance in influencing how teachers teach and how they influence the daily interactions we have with children, colleagues, administrators, parents, and community members. Philosophy traditionally is divided into three central areas of metaphysics, epistemology, and axiology that directly influence teaching theory and practice. Each of these branches tends to center on questions that shape core beliefs about life, and for the teacher, about how student and teacher interactions may occur.

Metaphysics is concerned with the nature of reality in its purest sense. This philosophy centers its discussions on questions like: What is real? What is the nature of existence? What is the meaning of life? Metaphysical issues or beliefs can have a particularly strong influence on teachers and their reactions to specific classroom situations. Teachers may view students as basically good, so they may interpret their students' actions and intentions as motivated by good rather than bad behavior. If a teacher views students as inherently bad, the teacher may interpret students' intentions as motivated by bad behavior. Each of these interpretations can have an enormous impact on classroom atmosphere and personal beliefs about specific situations. Obviously, our response as teachers can have a lasting impact on students.

Morrison (2009, 330) asks us to consider the following scenario: A student comes to you with a complaint that she is being bullied. Is your first impulse to sympathize with her, or is it to criticize her for not standing up for herself? Is it your job as an instructor to be a counselor and friend to the student, or merely an instructor? What is the role of the teacher, and how will you adapt to your beliefs about that role? How much of your personal background and experience will influence and shape your philosophy and response?

The discussion of the nature of knowledge and how knowledge is acquired is a central concern of the second major branch of philosophy, *epistemology*. Basic questions that surround epistemological discussions might include: How does knowing take place? How do we define knowledge? How is knowledge acquired? How do we decide what knowledge should be taught? Understanding epistemological beliefs is important to teachers because all teachers have embedded beliefs about how students acquire knowledge and how they learn best.

It would not be uncommon for teachers to stress the knowledge and beliefs that support their own background and experience. However, it is clearly evident that we should consider knowledge from other sources and backgrounds and additional experiential evidence from sources of authority. Students come to know the world and build upon their knowledge base through experiences, by sources of authority, through reason, through intuition, and through actively constructing their own world of knowledge.

Axiology, the branch of philosophy that addresses human conduct and beauty or ethics, plays a central role in the decisions that teachers make concerning curriculum, class discussions and activities, and daily interactions that teachers have with their students. Questions that involve issues of values, beliefs, ethical behavior, and issues of good, evil, and beauty are central to a teacher's own personal development, attitude, and outlook on life. These questions might include: What values are most important? Whose values are most important? How should we relate to and get along with others? What constitutes beauty? All of these questions would be central axiological questions.

Although teachers are guided by personal and professional ethics in interactions with children, ethical questions and moral beliefs continually guide and influence teachers' personal choices both in and out of the classroom. In today's world with concerns of international events, war and violence, substance abuse, teenage pregnancy, economic issues, and various other social issues, local communities expect schools and teachers in general to be the guardians of appropriate and acceptable behavior and conduct. Much of this is defined by the local community, rather than a preset definition of appropriate behavior. Values of honesty, respect for others, and the support of the general welfare of children are constant themes. Teachers need to understand these expectations when they pursue the teaching profession.

Under philosophy's main branches of metaphysics, epistemology, and axiology, several specific educational philosophies tend to have a major influence on educational practice, curriculum, and how teachers interact with their students in the classroom.

Perennialism

Perennialism, which grew out of idealism, means "everlasting." In a broad sense, the perennialist believes in everlasting knowledge—that knowledge has always endured and will continue to endure until the end of time. Originally developed by the former president of the University of Chicago, Robert Maynard Hutchins (1889–1977), in the early 1900s, it is an old educational theory that continued to shape the development of European and American universities until the late nineteenth century. Based upon what came to be known as the Great Books Curriculum, Hutchins focused on the concept that truth is perennial and enduring, and suggested, "Education implies teaching. Teaching implies knowledge. Knowledge is truth. Truth is everywhere the same. Hence education should be everywhere the same" (Sarte, 1978, 98). Reading and discussing the great works of Socrates, Plato, Homer, Melville, Thoreau, Darwin, and others would be typical of this curriculum. The role, then, of educators and schools would be to focus on the search for, and the dissemination of, the unchanging truths that humans (and, therefore, authors and philosophers) have discovered over the centuries. Mortimer Adler (1901–2001) continued Hutchins' work and is often referred to as a neoperennialist in that he gave new life to the perennialist perspective by encouraging the study of thought-provoking literature and ideas to the general public, and specifically at all grade levels within school classrooms.

Perennialists emphasize the authority of the teacher in the relationship between teacher and student and within the classroom environment. Since teachers are knowledgeable people of impeccable character, as perennialists insist they must be, they should take charge of the classroom and command the learning process in the direction of the intended outcome. Students may question ideas and concepts, as perennialists would encourage and in fact require critical thinking, but students would not be allowed to challenge the teacher's authority. The concepts of a democratic classroom and "student voice" would be discouraged in favor of a stronger focus on a common curriculum for all students with an emphasis on gaining existing knowledge, reasoning critically about human affairs and moral principles, and learning to value past recognized masterpieces of literature and philosophical perspectives. The work and beliefs of Hutchins and Adler, as well as other contemporary educators and philosophers that support Adler's *Paideia Proposal* (1982) of a contemporary revival of perennialism, continue to create discussion and controversy in education reform circles.

The central concern with perennialism remains a question of potential elitism, where only the brightest and most socioeconomically privileged students benefit from this form of curriculum and learning environment. Can we attempt to educate children as if they are all alike, where all knowledge and experiences are expected to be infinitely the same? If so, where does this leave the student who has experienced much more diverse background experiences in terms of race, ethnicity, religion, and limited monetary support? Those in the perennialist camp continue to suggest that children are inherently the same and that all deserve the same excellent education as defined by the great "thinkers" of our time. It is difficult to counter the potential socioeconomic, gender, and cultural bias that, at least on the surface, perennialism would tend to support.

Essentialism

Essentialism has had a major influence on American elementary and secondary schools and maintains that there is a common body of knowledge that all students need to learn to function effectively in society and, ultimately, to become productive and participatory citizens in their communities. This philosophy began as a reactionary effort to what some considered the decline of intellectual and moral standards within the public school institutions. William C. Bagley (1874–1946) founded the Essentialistic Education Society with the effort to promote essentialist ideas. Most essentialists recommend that students learn an academic-based core of knowledge with its roots tied to reading, writing, and mathematics, particularly in the elementary school years. Essentialists tend to focus on what they define as an intellectual curriculum, rather than a curriculum focused on growth and development.

As the name implies, essentialism promotes the learning of essential skills that can be agreed upon by Western cultural knowledge, and provides sole instruction, learning, and control in the classroom by advocating respect for the teacher, the authority in the classroom. The role of education, schools, and teachers is to teach essential skills and the traditional academic subjects with the goal of mastery education. In the essentialist classroom, the teacher is the authority of the subject in the field, and the explicit teaching of traditional Western values is encouraged.

With the back-to-basics essentialist approach, the late twentieth century has seen a vast increase in standardized testing, with a dominant emphasis on comparing students and schools against one another and the sole indicator of success being "test score indicators" generated on a particular day of the year. The enormous amount of current standards, accountability, and standardized testing at both the state and federal levels is a direct result of essentialist curriculum, where basic academic core knowledge is easily assessed and where students, schools, and school districts can be compared swiftly and efficiently.

As a result, legislative mandates such as No Child Left Behind have begun to consume the educational environment with threats of accountability and school closures. E. D. Hirsch, former professor of English, and William Bennett, former secretary of education during the second term of the Reagan administration, as well as other contemporary advocates for essentialism and broad academic testing (Chester Finn, Diane Ravitch, etc.), continue to support an educational philosophy dominated by a core-essentialist curriculum. Certainly authors like Darling-Hammond (2004), Kohn (2004a), Kozol (1991), Meier (2004), Ohanian (1999), Sizer (2004), Wood (2004), and countless others have difficulty with the current standards and assessment movement, suggesting that it continues to become an increasingly difficult task to come to a consensus on what is essential and what is not. For essentialists, however, a back-to-basics approach form of education is seen as key for the United States to become more productive and competitive in the world economy. As a result, testing is essential, accountability is mandated, and the philosophy of the teacher as the authority in the classroom who insists on discipline and order is essential to maintaining and encouraging traditional values in students. Cornerstone Western values such as the support of traditional moral concepts of honesty, respect, integrity, obedience, discipline, hard work, etc., are as essential to the orderly operation of schools as they are to the very existence of society.

Progressivism
In the 1930s, John Dewey looked into traditional classrooms and saw passivity, rigidity, and uniformity locked into place. Teachers were the dispensers of knowledge and took their places at the front of the classroom. Students were the receivers of knowledge and took their places in the rear (Newman, 2006, 242). Often called the father of progressivism, John Dewey did not approve of a factory-like model of school classrooms and felt that schools should not be places where teachers dictated orders and where students sat, listened, learned, and obeyed grudgingly. Dewey felt that schools should be places of participatory learning where students were actively engaged in learning and where teachers served as mentors and guides.

Dewey rejected traditional learning, where perhaps knowledge and truth were passed from one generation to the next, and instead promoted learning opportunities that were for the present generation. In the progressive model, experiential learning and hands-on interaction with the environment were key. Students were not simply receptacles or buckets that learning facts and knowledge was poured into, but rather active organisms that needed to learn by doing. Much of the progressive movement was based upon Dewey's view of democracy (Dewey, 1916), where he felt that the essence of democracy was people working together cooperatively to find solutions to common problems and problems of current society.

For critics of progressivism, their interpretations of this educational philosophy suggested that it was becoming no more than a collection of "catch" phrases or slogans like "learning by doing," "doing with Dewey," "educating the whole child," and "teaching students not subjects." Opportunities to build upon their natural inclination to explore and discover gave students greater freedom to examine topics of their own interest and to build upon their instincts to inquire, examine, and discover as they learned.

Many contemporary educational practices today are based on Dewey-ian progressive ideas. Cooperative learning, multi-age grouping, arranging rooms into interest and activity centers that enable students to choose what they will learn and how they will learn it, curricula that emphasize students' self-esteem, and the teaching of conflict resolution techniques for getting along with others are all examples and basic byproducts of the progressive movement (Morrison, 2009, 343). The progressive classroom became a child-centered classroom where much of student learning was independent and self-directed and where collaborative efforts were engaged in as learning-by-doing activities.

Social Reconstructivism, Critical Theory, and Postmodern Beliefs

A society-centered form of progressivism called social reconstructivism also began to emerge in the late 1930s that had a strong political demeanor. George Counts, a Teachers College professor at the time, called upon teachers to become agents and leaders of social change. By taking a stand on prominent controversial social issues of the time, teachers would be, in effect, facilitating students to be prepared for the emerging society. Social reconstructivists, therefore, embraced a great desire to use the schools and the classrooms to engineer a new—and, in their opinion, a potentially better—society for the future. Building on progressive pedagogy, social reconstructivists continued to become more left-of-center in terms of their political beliefs, and therefore predictably drew the fire, and at times the disillusionment, of educationally and politically conservative citizens. In fact, conservative critics have argued that social reconstructivists' writings are nothing more than indicators of a left-wing conspiracy to control the schools (Newman, 2006).

Contemporary social reconstructivists have begun to embrace a new term often referred to today as *critical theory*. Although some would argue that social reconstructivism and critical theory are not the same, many of the issues, agendas, and/or philosophies that each group supports have similar roots and future goals. As each of the names imply, they believe that teachers, students, and their schools can each play a key role in reconstructing society and supporting an effort toward a new social order that potentially will result in more democratic and effective communities (Morrison, 2009, 344).

By focusing on the social effort to empower the powerless and the attempt to transform existing social inequalities and injustices, contemporary critical theorists like Henry Giroux (2004), Stanley Aronowitz (1985), Peter McLaren (McLaren and Lankshear 1993), and Paulo Freire (1970), to name a few, are beginning to have an impact on university faculty and colleges of education, while the writings of those like Alfie Kohn (2004b), Jonathon

Kozol (1991), Deborah Meier (2004), Susan Ohanian (1999), Sonia Nieto (2003), and others are reaching even larger audiences.

Although in reality critical theory is a contemporary extension of social reconstructivism, true critical theorists resolve to help students, teachers, and those of disenfranchised backgrounds (underrepresented minority groups and the economically poor or disadvantaged) escape from what they perceive as oppression by using progressive pedagogy and radical politics. Critical theorists recognize and acknowledge the influence of Dewey, Counts, and other progressives, but they also suggest that their goals of empowering the disadvantaged and transforming society are more explicitly political than the goals of Dewey and his contemporaries.

Postmodern theory has grown even more sensitive to the influence of social class, race, ethnicity, and gender. These theorists would suggest that these specific factors strongly impact how individuals perceive reality because every perception is shaped by prior experience. One example would be that women and men see and perceive things differently because they construct reality differently in their minds, based upon their past experiences. They would also suggest that, unfortunately, traditional academic scholarship (and schools and their curricula) have ignored these differences and that traditional standards and expectations have a significant Western, white, male, and economically privileged perspective.

Certainly social reconstructivists, critical theorists, and post modern philosophers whose thinking is perhaps at least partially influenced by Marxism believe that schools often serve the interests of the dominant socioeconomic group of the state and tend to perpetuate the capitalistic system (Morrison, 2009, 344). Whether you agree or disagree with the role that education and schools should play in the deconstruction and reform of our current educational system and society, critical theorists certainly encourage a deeper analysis of and reflection on contemporary thought and current practice.

From a philosophy that supports learning as "random wanderings in the woods" to more of a critical perspective where the clear goal is to challenge and reform our current educational structure and political climate, the essence of teaching and learning remains a difficult concept to define. In this opening chapter, the goal has been to provide a foundation for the discussion of teaching and learning, and in a historical sense to explore how these concepts have been defined and how they continue to be debated. The ultimate essence of teaching, however, is the ability to share one's passion for learning and discovery with students. It is all about mentoring unselfishly and giving of oneself, despite the struggle and potential hardships, and the limited financial rewards. It may also be about encouraging educational, political, and social change and social justice within the minds and futures of our students.

Essential to teaching, leadership is the topic of the next chapter, where the discussion continues in the venue of leadership in the classroom and in the school setting. The case will eventually be made that understanding the blend of teaching and leadership around the role of service to the school community is ultimately the first step in truly becoming a teacher who is a servant leader.

CHAPTER TWO

~

The Teacher as Leader

The older type of instruction tended to treat the teacher as a dictatorial ruler: The newer type sometimes treats the teacher as a negligible fact, almost as an evil, though a necessary one. In reality, the teacher is the intellectual leader of a social group. He [she] is a leader, not in virtue of official position, but because of wider and deeper knowledge and matured experience. The supposition that the principle of freedom confers liberty upon the pupils, but that the teacher is outside of its range and must abdicate all leadership is merely silly.

—John Dewey (LW 8:337)

When we traditionally think of leadership, specifically school leadership, our definition tends to center on the specific administrator of the school. Often, the principal, central office administrator, or even a superintendent has the charge of leading students and their teachers toward academic and personal achievement. Rightfully so, school administrators have the charge of leading their staffs and students to excellence and being held accountable for their guidance, mentorship, and ability to inspire. They are, in the truest sense, the instructional leaders who set the stage for a positive learning environment and for progress and reform in classrooms. This chapter, however, focuses on leadership within the perspective of the teacher in the classroom, where the teacher is the guide of the learning process and ultimately responsible for instilling a passion for learning and discovery in the classroom.

In 1934, W. B. Munro suggested six personal qualities or characteristics that he felt were essential if a person were to play the role of leader:

1. Unusual sensitiveness to the strength and direction of social and industrial tendencies.
2. Acute and quick perception of possible courses of conduct with plans for quick action.
3. Facility in compromise.
4. Ability to make personal contacts easily.
5. Dramatic ability; the ability to use voice and pen dramatically for the purpose of emotionally influencing people.
6. Courage.

Therefore, whether a president, senator, judge, military general, school administrator, tribal chief, sultan, or classroom teacher, the leader of an organization or a group of people must possess a sensitivity to the needs and direction of their constituents, be able to make quick and accurate decisions, possess the ability to compromise, and be able to influence people with a courage and confidence without crossing the line of arrogance.

A few years later, Thorndike (1940) asserted another general list of fourteen characteristics of leadership that also included a genuine kindness and a sense of brotherhood, great energy, character, and guarded sincerity and honesty. Kraines (1947) further suggested that leadership is a function of "essential qualities" that also included true social interest, intelligence, energy, and courage. Perhaps one of the earliest books that had a profound impact on individuals who study leadership was written in 1935 by Ordway Tead. In *The Art of Leadership*, he lists ten paramount qualities of leadership:

1. Physical and nervous energy.
2. A sense of purpose and direction.
3. Enthusiasm.
4. Friendliness and affection.
5. Integrity.
6. Technical mastery.
7. Decisiveness.
8. Intelligence.
9. Teaching skill.
10. Faith.

Though often referred to as trait theory, the likes of Munro, Thorndike, Kraines, Tead, and others perhaps fall short in their attempts to describe the specific traits of effective leaders. At the least, Tead begins to add to the list with fresh leadership concepts of helping people achieve purposes and goals that are theirs, and noting that leadership does actually function within a matrix involving purposes, values, and faith. Gouldner (1950) criticized trait or personal-qualities theory, suggesting:

1. A list of personal qualities or traits fails to suggest the relative importance of any one specific trait.
2. A list of personal qualities or traits may not be mutually exclusive.
3. Lists of leadership traits do not present any suggestion of those that are essential to ascent to positions of leadership, essential to the maintenance of leadership, or essential to maintaining current status.
4. Lists of traits are largely descriptive; there is little or no attention given to how such traits were acquired.
5. The traits assigned to leadership have been developed, to a large extent, in terms of traits of particular leaders.

In spite of the broad acceptance of trait or personal-qualities theory for centuries to describe or explain leadership, these theories have limitations, as Gouldner has suggested previously, in that although some of these traits may be common to all leaders, they may also be possessed by non-leaders. In addition, leadership qualities that are effective in one situation may not be effective in another (Weber and Weber, 1961). Tead (1935) may have suggested that many of the qualities listed previously are qualities that we would expect or seek to develop in all citizens, not just in those with leadership roles. Groups and circumstances differ in a variety of ways; therefore, actions required for the achievement of certain goals in one situation may differ widely from those that are essential in another unique situation.

Whether being a military leader on the battlefield, the leader of a growing nation, the CEO of a major corporation, or an educational leader (as an administrator or classroom teacher), in this brief introduction of leadership I have intentionally used older sources and references to begin the initial leadership discussion. The goal is to begin to set the stage for an exploration of contemporary ways to consider leadership, specifically within school settings. No two schools are just alike. No school faculties and personnel are just alike. Similarly, no classroom of students is just alike. Each has its own personality, characteristics, and specific needs that require a dynamic exchange of ideas and reflection among teachers and administrators and among those that will be led.

Contemporary Theories of Leadership

In 1995, Howard Gardner wrote *Leading Minds: An Anatomy of Leadership*, where he proposed a theory of leadership that focused on the mind with a deliberate attempt to explore the cognitive qualities of extraordinary leaders. Gardner not only focused on the mind of the leader, but on the mind of the leader's followers as he examined the lives and leadership capacity of J. Robert Oppenheimer, Eleanor Roosevelt, Martin Luther King Jr., Mahatma Gandhi, and others from a cognitive perspective. He also differentiated between fundamental leaders who exhibited leadership within a specific domain (i.e. Einstein in the area of physics) and those who exhibited leadership within a wider society. Within a specific domain or discipline, one assumes that the audience is already as sophisticated as the leader in communicating by sharing stories and visions with experts. In contrast, leaders who expect to lead or reorient a political entity, like a nation or a broad-based institution, are not dealing with experts but with individuals who bring ordinary, relatively undisciplined frames of mind to the table (Gardner, 1995).

Gardner's cognitive approach or exploration of leadership departs from a behaviorist perspective that typically focused on observable, overt actions, and from a psychoanalyst perspective where personality and motivation were perhaps the central theme. From a cognitive perspective, leadership is represented by how ideas, thoughts, and mental representations are stored, accessed, combined, remembered, rearranged, or distorted by the operations of the human mind.

In Gardner's view, the study of the phenomenon of leadership from a cognitive orientation might ask the following questions: What are the ideas (or stories) of the leader? How have they developed? How are they communicated? How are they understood and misunderstood? How do they interact with other stories? How do key ideas or stories affect the thoughts, feelings, and behaviors of other individuals? In most earlier and current psychological studies of leadership, researchers focused on the personality of the leader, while Gardner's work represents a shift from personality to the cognitive aspect of leadership.

While there is some merit to understanding a leader's personal needs, early life experiences, and relationships to other individuals, Gardner proposes that personality alone cannot explain the particular course called for by a leader or the degree of success achieved with various audiences (1995).

Therefore, a cognitive approach—the mental structures activated by leaders and their followers—completes the descriptive nature of true leadership.

Effective leadership often depends on the leader's ability and courage to face the facts in a particular situation, interpret the facts or even data appropriately in light of the situation's requirements, and follow the course of action that the facts dictate. Management of a multitude of these variables is crucial, but it is important to understand that leadership is more than management. It therefore becomes a limiting factor to think of administration and leadership in strictly operational terms. Educational leaders need to be able to have the capacity or the ability and desire to encourage the tools of learning, scientific principles, facts, and techniques for mediating conflicting interests and value judgments, and the ability to make private and public decisions at moments of vital concern. Leadership is about creating a vision, working with those both outside and inside the organization and inspiring others. In contrast, management is about executing the vision. Strong leaders are not only visionary in having the ability to lead, but they also have the capacity to manage and execute strategies that can make the vision a reality.

From a democratic framework, school leadership should meet the four basic needs of man, namely (1) the freedom to make inquiry and to initiate action; (2) a sense of belonging to a cohesive, worthy group of people engaged in a significant enterprise; (3) a feeling for the professionalization of the career of teaching; and (4) a sense of genuine success in building an educational program that really produces the growth of children intellectually, psychologically, physically, and emotionally (Weber and Weber, 1961).

In his introduction to *The Art of School Leadership*, Thomas Hoerr (2005, 1) suggests, "Strong leaders are artists. They inspire, applaud, chastise, steer, and stand on the side. They create, monitor, reinforce, encourage, and stand in the back. Yes, sometimes they stand in the front too. They recognize that it is their responsibility to help create a setting in which each individual can flourish and everyone can grow. Strong leaders understand that leadership is about relationships."

The description of school leaders as artists suggests that there is no one specific formula, no particular policy, and no exact set of procedures that will work with everyone, in every situation, in every school. Like the artist, the evaluation of a work of art is subjective and very much dependent on one's individual perspective. School and classroom leadership cannot follow a stir-and-serve recipe. Often, the very qualities that we desire in teachers and administrators—passion, creativity, and a thirst for independence—can make it difficult for them to share, to work toward a common goal, and to be good teammates (Hoerr, 2005).

In the 1980s, leadership (or the lack of it) became the named excuse for a myriad of national problems (Razik and Swanson, 2010). In the 1990s and early 2000s, a lack of leadership in the United States appeared to be at fault for our decline in the global economy; at the same time, leadership was a potential vehicle to restore our lost power and prestige (Rost, 1991). Even as early as 1978, Burns maintained that "the crisis of leadership today is the mediocrity or irresponsibility of so many men and women in power" (1). In terms of leadership in schools, current and contemporary educational theorists (Sergiovanni, 1994; Fullan, 2005; Hargreaves, 2005; Covington, 2007; Rogers-Healey, 2003; Mackenzie, 2007; Sarason, 2004) offer a changing vision of school leadership that focuses on a wide variety of topics, including the development of professional learning communities, leadership from the center rather than a top-down approach, sustainable leadership for change, the empowerment of females in the leadership role, moral leadership, and a greater emphasis on relationship building among all stakeholders (including the administration, students, teachers, and their parents).

Despite all of the literature that continues to redefine the role of school administrators and school leadership, the reality is that in a world of global change, ever-changing technology, and rapid access to immediate information, a growing population of world workers needs new or changed abilities and skills, and our students need to be well-prepared to be productive citizens in this new environment. In terms of leadership, our perspective on how it can be defined, how teachers at the ground level can sustain it, and how we can keep it within the scope of service becomes a key ingredient in the cycle of supporting students, families, and communities.

If we return to the original list proposed by Tead in 1935, we can begin to gain a sense of not only leadership from an administrative standpoint, but also from a teacher's leadership perspective within the classroom and the school building. From Tead's perspective, leadership qualities should contain the following concepts. Within the classroom specifically, leadership is essentially the art of helping students to define and achieve their goals and purposes, and also functions within a matrix that involves purposes, values, and faith.

Physical and Nervous Energy

Those who rise in any marked way above the mass of men have conspicuously more drive, more sheer endurance, greater vigor of body and mind than the average person. The leader's effectiveness, in the first instance, depends upon his or her basic constitutional strength and robustness. Expanding on Tead's words, the classroom teacher leader must possess a sense of physical and nervous energy. This energy must be perceived by students and colleagues, not necessarily in a physical sense, but by an energy for the subject and for working with students. The kindergarten teacher must have the same energy, passion, and excitement for creating a snow scene on card stock with cotton balls and glue sticks as her kindergarten students.

By the same token, the high school math teacher must have a sense of urgency and excitement in deriving the quadratic formula, and somehow she must allow her students to also see this energy of mathematical creativity. A dispassionate teacher with no energy and excitement will never be able to inspire his or her students toward the same passion for creativity and learning.

A Sense of Purpose and Direction

A teacher leader needs to have a sense of purpose and direction and needs to be able to communicate this to his or her students. Students need to understand the direction and focus for the day, and in the long term, need to understand the goals of learning on a larger scale. In today's world at the elementary school level, we may call this "seat work" or "bell work," but this early class activity sets the stage for purpose and direction for the rest of the hour or the complete day. This does not mean that teachers are late to class or that they spend time in the hallway after the start of class drinking their morning coffee while chatting with their colleague across the hall. When class begins, teachers are on task with a sense of purpose, and they convey this sense of purpose to their students in both verbal and nonverbal form with their actions and demeanor.

Enthusiasm

The effective teacher leader feels deeply, is emotionally primed, and has a power to summon and elevate the desires of others that wholly transcends the rational level. Good leaders are enthusiasts. They are, in a measure, possessed, caught up, instruments of a cause or power that uses them (Tead, 1935). Extraordinary teachers have a great passion for four things: learning, the content they are teaching, their students, and effective instruction (Stephenson, 2001). They believe in—almost to a flaw—their work, the people they serve, and their mission as teachers. If teachers lack enthusiasm for any of these four, their chances for extraordinary success are unlikely.

Being possessed means being consumed. Being possessed by teaching, your subject, and those you work with creates a contagious enthusiasm within the classroom.

Friendliness and Affection (Personal Relationships)

Although Tead originally labeled this quality as friendliness and affection, perhaps a better definition by today's standards centers on the development of a positive rapport and personal relationships. Teacher leadership means a mobilization of emotional power, enthusiasm, and passion, and each of these qualities is translated into relationships to both students and colleagues. Students need to believe that teachers care about them and their success as students and individuals.

The concept of unconditional positive regard holds a key place in the development of relationships, regardless of whether we think of this in a student-teacher framework or from a teacher-leader perspective. The extraordinary teacher has an unconditional positive regard for students, regardless of ethnicity, socioeconomic status, English speaking ability, religion, political preference, homelessness, preferences of gender, learning disabilities, or alternative lifestyles, and has the ability and desire to develop positive relationships and rapport with every student (and their parents) that walks into their classroom.

Integrity

Students must be able to trust their teachers. They want to feel that their interests are safe in the teacher leader's hands and that the teacher will not betray them or sell them out, or more importantly, get tired of serving them. The concept of integrity may be difficult to define, but it begins with a sense of discipline, unconditional support, patience, graciousness, diplomacy, and the enthusiasm for knowledge. Integrity does not mean the absence of firmness and high expectations, but rather a commitment to excellence, high standards, and expectations for self and others, along with a temperament for flexibility as we value personal and learning differences.

Professional athletes will often state that they have no desire to be role models to a younger generation, thereby excusing their sometimes inappropriate behavior and actions on and off the field of play. Whether we like it or not, teachers are role models. Our adherence to a code of ethical principles within the teaching profession sets the stage for integrity within the profession and gives the community, parents, and our students a confidence in our ability to nurture and guide their children.

Technical Mastery

In terms of technology and technical mastery, the teacher leader must possess enough of a grasp of the most effective and latest trends within their content area to provide wise guidance and instructional practice to their students. This means that the teacher has mastery—or at the least, a working knowledge—of the latest advancements in software, distance learning, electronic media, electronic information gathering, learning tools, and innovative learning trends. As the educational content area continues to expand and develop, effective teachers remain abreast of the latest and most innovative teaching techniques and pedagogy to assist them in preparing students for the current workforce and higher education.

Decisiveness

Decisiveness is sometimes thought of as a peremptory quality of rapid and perhaps intuitive character, yet the appearance of rapidity is often deceptive. The teacher leader, by his or her immersion in the facts of his or her situation, is frequently able to make a wise decision with what appears to be great speed. But what appears to be an intuitive flash is often the result of deep reflection, or of an incubation of ideas that have been growing for some time (Tead, 1935). The systematic development and habit of thinking through problems and situations quickly allows teachers to move forward with correct and decisive decisions about curricula, instructional processes, pedagogical concerns, and student behavior so that the classroom remains an environment of focus, direction, and student confidence in the teacher and in their own potential.

Intelligence

Intelligence, for Tead, was defined by pure knowledge of the subject area. He even stated that one should not assume a leadership role with which one's intelligence is not able to cope, and that no leader can rise higher than his [her] mentality will allow (Tead, 1935). Certainly in the years that followed, we have come to understand that intelligence is not just defined by our content area. We do need to ensure that teacher leaders are competent in their subject matter before they assume the responsibility of the instructional leader in the classroom. But in today's world, intelligence is far more than content. Intelligence involves knowledge of human behavior and relationships; understanding of human psychology, motivation, self-esteem, self-confidence, and emotions; and understanding the impact that socioeconomic and other environmental factors can have on students and their learning. It also represents an understanding of the physical community and neighborhoods that your school serves, as well as the classroom community that you and your students hope to create. With the current requirements of No Child Left Behind legislation in assessment and accountability, it might also mean that the teacher leader has a clear understanding of national, state, and local district goals in the form of standards and expectations. Finally, intelligence also means that teachers understand and have a sense of what students need at the moment, what they have accomplished, perhaps personal circumstances they have overcome in the past, and the understanding of differentiated ways to help them develop future goals and personal success.

Teaching Skill

Teaching skill is critical for the teacher leader. One can possess much of the practical "intelligence" listed above without having the skill or ability to assist students through experiences that can bring about a change in mind and motive. Tasks such as holding a classroom's interest despite multiple learning capacities and levels of student receptivity, multi-tasking while juggling a multitude of variables and interruptions, attending to student needs while focusing on your personal instructional goals, and balancing demands from parents and requests from administrators—these all require a multiplicity of abilities.

The key skill is for teachers to have the capacity to instructionally energize their classrooms and to have the knowledge and desire to present information using multiple formats, if necessary, for the sake of a diversity of learning levels and styles. The teacher remains the instructional leader of the classroom, regardless of your preference for a direct instructional approach or one where students explore, create, and discover their own knowledge base. The teacher is still responsible for differentiated instruction and providing a pedagogical framework that is sound and that ultimately supports student learning.

Faith

The idea of faith is not considered, necessarily, as a religious experience in terms of the teaching profession, although many have been known to pray daily for patience and for spring break to arrive sooner rather than later! In the teacher leader context, faith is seen as a belief in the effort that a focus toward the good (however this is defined) can yield appreciable results. Faith in the teaching profession and the learning process is more of an attitude that the objective of learning and discovering new information has appreciable value. This faith in learning might also support other values important to other life activities and future goals. In essence, extraordinary teacher leaders have a steadfast faith in their students' ability to learn and grow despite their circumstances, and in their own abilities to accept their students as they are and assist them to move beyond their current state of development.

Hoerr (2005) remains steadfast that school leadership is all about the development of relationships. The best supervisors and leaders support teamwork and collegiality, value diversity, and encourage everyone around them to grow. In the classroom, as well, a teacher who is a good leader has the ability to develop and promote positive relationships among students and between students and themselves.

Being an intellectual leader in the classroom is indispensable for the teacher. Being a developer and encourager of relationships is a precursor to this intellectual gain that we hope to accomplish with our students. If teachers don't create a positive learning environment in their classrooms, in which relationships flourish and students are free to explore and investigate without concern for imperfection or failure, they have lost their sense of what teaching is about and have not provided leadership to their students in the establishment of classroom communities ripe for engagement and participation in the art of thinking and learning.

CHAPTER THREE

~

The Teacher as
Servant and Steward

It is not the critic who counts; not the man who points out how the strong man stumbled, or where the doer of deeds could have done better. The credit belongs to the man who is actually in the arena; whose face is marred by dust and sweat and blood; who strives valiantly; who errs and comes up short again and again. Who knows the great enthusiasms, the great devotions, and spends himself in a worthy cause. Who at the best knows in the end the triumph of high achievement; and who at the worst, if he fails, at least fails while daring greatly. So that his place shall never be with those cold and timid souls who know neither victory nor defeat.

—Theodore Roosevelt, *Citizen in a Republic Speech*
at the Sorbonne, Paris (April 23, 1910)

Although the central purpose of a teacher is that of instructional leader in the classroom, a teacher is more than a director or guide of curriculum and the provider of the daily task of learning new information. Above all, the servant leader is a servant first, and is driven by the inner compassion and the conscious choice of serving others in a variety of capacities. This differs sharply from one who is a leader first, perhaps due to the need to assert an unusual power or drive for control over others. The leader-first and the servant-first are two extreme types. Between them there are shadows and blends that are part of the infinite variety of human nature (Greenleaf, 1977).

Stewardship, although similar to the concept of servant, is a term that suggests that someone is deeply accountable for the outcomes of a particular institution or a particular group of people, without acting to define purpose for others, control others, or take care of others (Block, 1993). In essence, stewardship is the willingness to be accountable for the well-being of others, rather than controlling others. It is accountability without control or compliance. The goal of choosing service and stewardship over self-interest is antithetical to much of today's world, where corporate greed, self-interest, and self-preservation appear to be monumental. When we choose service and stewardship over self-interest, we are basically saying that we are willing to be held deeply accountable without choosing to control the world around us. Governance structures and leadership styles aimed at consistency, predictability, and control work well in stable, predictable environments where all intervening variables can be controlled. Unfortunately, schools and classrooms are not stable, predictable environments, and teachers don't control the multitude of variables that impact students and their learning and growth. Ultimately, teaching is a service-oriented profession, and exceptional teachers choose their career initially because they enjoy working with children and young adults and they have a great desire to serve and to have an impact on the next generation.

Encompassing service and stewardship within the classroom not only lays the initial groundwork for a positive learning environment, but it also sets the stage for a more productive community of learners, each supporting one another as a matter of choice rather than manipulation or control.

The Teacher as Servant

In the opening quote to this chapter, Theodore Roosevelt states, "The credit belongs to the man who is actually in the arena; whose face is marred by dust and sweat and blood," which implies that the servant leader is one with experiences, one who has rolled up their sleeves and is not afraid to get their hands dirty, maimed, and marred. It is difficult to lead from outside of the arena, and eventually, those in the midst of "battle" will lose respect for and confidence in those who have not helped to dig the trench. From an educational and teacher's perspective, John Dewey supported the belief that students need to develop a view of life that helps them get beyond personal interests to consider the interests of others, including the people in their schools, communities, nation, and world (Simpson, Jackson, and Aycock, 2005). As Dewey stated: "So I appeal to teachers in the face of every hysterical wave of emotion, and of every subtle appeal of sinister class interest, to remember that they above all others are the consecrated servants of democratic ideas in which alone this country is truly a distinctive nation—ideas of friendly and helpful intercourse between all and the equipment of every individual to serve the community by his [her] own best powers in his [her] own best way" (MW 10:210).

The central focus of service for the educator from a Deweyian perspective is the promotion of a culture within our schools and classrooms that takes into consideration the importance of living democratically. We as teachers are not simply engaged in teaching our content and individuals, but in the proper formation of a social life. Dewey believed all teachers should consider themselves as social servants, set apart for the maintenance of proper social order and the securing of social growth. In his writing *My Pedagogic Creed* (1897), Dewey felt that as social servants, teachers are always prophets of the true God and the usherers in of the true kingdom of God (EW 5:95). Dewey would suggest that as teachers and servants, we should commit to building, sustaining, expanding, and refining a democratic society.

As servant teachers, not only do we serve our students and our immediate school community, but we also strategically build and develop democratic classrooms and encourage a life of democratic living and principles among our students. This focus would also begin to suggest that serving and living democratically is counter to much of what we see emphasized in the world today, which encourages decisions based on capitalistic ventures. Schools and teachers have a difficult, delicate, and challenging role to play in that we often are working against a counter-culture that supports undemocratic philosophies and goals. Although the direct definition of democracy might be one of a government in which the supreme power is vested in the people and exercised by them directly or indirectly through a system of representation, democratic classrooms can borrow from this definition as teachers develop their role as servant, teacher, and leader of a community of learners where everyone is served and every student has an equal voice and opportunity for development and accomplishment.

If democratic classroom environments can be encouraged by the role of the teacher in a servant capacity, how then does the teacher actually become a servant of the students, the classroom, and the greater school community? A portion of the answer to this question may lie in a perception of power, both from the teacher's perspective and from the perspective of the students that will be led. Ideally, someone else can have power over us or we can have power over them only to the degree that we agree, consciously or subconsciously, to enter into that relationship (Hoerr, 2005).

Most of us are uncomfortable with other people having power over us. Traditionally, the education profession has attracted people who do not seek a great deal of power and who hold a view—at least in a minor capacity—of service to others, namely students. Inherently, there is perhaps a negative connotation to the idea of power, but what matters most is how this power is used in the classroom and how it can be used to promote democratic principles and to develop a service-oriented environment.

Traditionally, the classic models of social power identified five different and unique views of power (French and Raven, 1959) and their potential impact on leadership and social influence. Typically, leaders may possess more than one type of power and may use them in combination with one another depending on circumstances and on the audience they hope to lead or influence. Not all of these types of power, however, would encourage democracy or support an environment that would set the stage for the teacher to be viewed as a servant leader.

Power Based on Rewards

Power based on rewards is essentially a behaviorist notion of the ability of someone to influence behavior based on some type of reward mechanism. The rewards can be tangible or intangible and most always are extrinsic in nature. When we compliment a child for good work on an assignment, we are not only complimenting them, but we are using the power of reward to reinforce past and current actions, which itself encourages similar future behavior. How students perceive this feedback (or reward) will have a significant impact on their motivation to pursue a future task. We could offer a reward of ice cream for making 100 percent on the Friday spelling test, but it is only perceived as a reward and motivating if the student likes ice cream. If the student has an aversion to ice cream, it is doubtful that this mechanism that the teacher sees as a reward will actually be seen as rewarding to the student.

Many researchers (Kohn, 1993; Csikszentmihalyi, 1990; Deci, 1971; Lepper, 1973) have warned of the dangers of the overuse of rewards and incentives in that they set the stage for inappropriate expectations and can actually decrease motivation, especially when the reward no longer exists. Although a supreme behaviorist like B. F. Skinner stated, "What a fascinating thing! Total control of a living organism" (1983, 400, 412), as educators we can also understand that children are not rats, dogs, or pigeons and at times it might not be wise to attempt to "control" their behavior with the promise of rewards. Gaining and using power based upon rewards is shallow and limited in its impact and does not place the teacher in a position of servant, but more in the position of a person who can control behavior with superficial reward mechanisms. The underlying question is, what happens to behavior when the reward is no longer present?

Power Based on Coercion

The reciprocal of power based on rewards is power based on the use of coercive tactics. The ability to punish or to remove rewards lies within the recesses of coercive power. As power based on rewards uses the "carrot on a stick" to make the donkey turn a certain direction, power based on coercion uses the threat of being "beaten by the stick" to direct the appropriate behavior. In classroom terms, we can use the reward of ice cream to encourage the score of 100 percent on the spelling test (power based on rewards), or we can use the threat of loss of playground time or after-school detention to also encourage this same 100 percent (power based on coercion). In either case, do students ever understand the importance of spelling or the value of accomplishment, or that proper spelling might help them to be a better writer someday, or do they simply react to a reward or punishment? Clearly the use of reward and coercive power has to be used appropriately if used at all, and perhaps it is best used coupled with a discussion of the reason for rewards and consequences.

Good behavior is important to encourage, not specifically with a reward system or the threat of punishment, but in a discussion with students of how we define "good behavior" and why it is important. If students take ownership of defining behavior and understand its value to themselves and others, the teacher has the chance of not being seen as the enforcer and punisher of broken rules, but more as a servant and facilitator of a positive classroom environment.

Power Based on Title and Position: Legitimate Power

Legitimate power is determined by an individual's official title or position. Often, in a specific hierarchical position, individuals have the "power" or authority to perform a certain task or are in the position of evaluating those that are lower in the hierarchy structure. This legitimate power is perhaps the weakest because we now live in an age where we tend to judge people based upon talent and skill rather than the specific position of authority they occupy. Barth referred to this as "positional power" (2004, 106), while Bolman and Deal noted that rarely will people provide their best effort and full cooperation when told to do so by an authority figure (2004, 184).

If we have legitimate power based upon our position, we can force change, conformity, or compliance, but seldom is this change long-lasting. In a school building structure, this power is often seen as a level of positional hierarchy where the principal, as a result of his or her title and responsibilities, maintains power over the teachers and supports staff who are often seen as subordinate. Likewise, teachers are higher in the positional hierarchy than their students, so a sense of power and control exists at multiple levels.

The issue of legitimate power can also become more complex, as it may take the form of horizontal structure rather than vertical. Some may attribute legitimate power based upon gender, age, or race. So, if I am an older, white male, I may be seen as having more power than a female, a younger person, or an individual with a background other than the majority race. This legitimate power may be real or it may be imagined, but the results are the same.

By way of position or title, we often feel either subordinate or superior to others, and therefore struggle with leading or following others based upon assumed authority. Although we can understand that the teacher is in a position of legitimate power within the classroom based upon a specific hierarchical structure, students may be more apt to give their best effort knowing that the teacher is a servant with the intent to assist them to achieve and grow, rather than use the power of position to "force" compliance.

Charismatic or Referent Power

Charismatic or referent power may be the most difficult to acquire and perhaps may be the least amenable to modification. The power that an individual has based on how others esteem or identify with them and their beliefs, values, and words can be powerful, and is most often related to personality characteristics. This type of power can also be related to both reward and coercive power in that at the least, the charismatic leader can be seen as a person who can potentially provide rewards to his or her followers.

We are drawn to the charisma, personality, and apparent charm of the individual, whether a youth gang leader set on destructive behaviors, or a senator, religious leader, president, or political leader who we think can lead us to greatness. Clearly John F. Kennedy, Ronald Reagan, Bill Clinton, Jesse Jackson, and most recently Barack Obama, despite representing various ends of the political spectrum, share or shared a degree and an abundance of referent power (Hoerr, 2005). However, other leaders and politicians over the years, for example, have had more difficulty with this "charisma" factor and have struggled to maintain their positions due to a lack of referent power.

Of all the forms of social power, referent power may arguably be the one that is the least likely to attain and the most difficult to define and develop. Most people can recognize this natural trait in an individual when they observe it but struggle with giving someone with this characteristic clear definition. Most would agree that someone either has "it" or not; we can distinguish "it" when we see "it" but struggle to give "it" a pure and clear description. Derived from charisma and personality, referent power is perhaps the least amenable to modification (Hoerr, 2005).

For the classroom teacher, the attribute of referent power can be a valuable characteristic, provided that teachers use their skills and personality to encourage students to achieve and grow based upon the students' own desires and personal goals. If we can allow and encourage students to assist us with creating a positive learning environment by making use of our own personality and philosophy of service to their needs, we eventually set the stage for them to have ownership of the outcome of their own learning, achievement, and future goals. Eventually we will no longer be their teacher or instructor, just as President Obama will eventually no longer be president. The ultimate goal is to use the referent power that we may possess as teachers to encourage an independence of learning within our students to the level that we have served their needs and set the stage for future achievement without the need of our assistance.

Expert Power

Power based on one's knowledge and experience is defined as expert power. When the plumber tells me that my house needs a new hot water tank or when my physician encourages me to undergo a medical procedure, I typically comply because I am not an expert in plumbing or medical issues. I often yield to their recommendations due to their expert power and their experience. Some might suggest that this type of power transcends hierarchy and role and other forms of power in that we respect wisdom and experience and follow suggestions based upon these attributes. In a similar fashion, students' parents may follow the recommendations about their children that come from a teacher or principal if they perceive these professionals as having expert power or knowledge.

The attribute of expert may be generated by the accumulation of academic degrees, a specific professional license, or a particular title we hold, but ideally it comes from true and authentic experiences. It is no wonder that in the past several years, the term or title of "auto mechanic" has changed to that of "service technician." Service technician has the ring of an expert title and perhaps is an indicator of more training, but at the least, it sounds like someone with more experience and technical expertise. The key indicator, however, is the question of whether the service technician can correctly diagnose my car's problem and replace the water pump if needed.

In schools, teachers and administrators can struggle with the balance of power and their desire to serve. Parents and students are often becoming more demanding, more critical, more sensitive, and even more educated in the ways of how schools operate. I have never had brain surgery or actually seen a surgeon perform this operation, so if I were told I needed this operation, I would most likely yield to their expertise and subject myself to this procedure and discomfort knowing they are the professionals and have the experience to be successful. In the world of teaching, we have all had teachers, both good and bad. Parents and teachers have had good experiences and those that were not very positive. We have personally seen and experienced teaching done well by experts, and teaching done poorly by individuals who really need to leave the profession as soon as possible due to their poor performance and the negative impact they have on children.

The unique challenge for educators—specifically the classroom teacher—is to understand the use of power, regardless of its derivation, and gain the ability to encourage a sense of shared power in the classroom and in our school buildings and community. In the truest sense, shared power is one that promotes environments that support social justice, basic freedoms, individual respect, personal safety, and classrooms that nurture democratic principles within our students. As Dewey stated, the implications for service that incorporates democracy for daily life include, among other ideals, the practice of nurturing in students:

- The tendency to encourage equal opportunity for the development of everyone.
- The predisposition to support freedom of lifestyle for everyone.
- The inclination to promote open communities among like- and unlike-minded peoples.
- The bent to develop cooperative activities for the common good.
- The disposition to seek resolution of disagreements by discussions and interactions.
- The willingness to work toward the basic needs of each person.
- The penchant to consider the interests and aspirations of everyone.
- The proclivity to support the growth of common and personal interests. (LW 14:226–228; MW 9:7–9)

Service and democracy need to be more than a list of external rules or laws. If our students remain unchanged in their attitudes, feelings, and thinking about our interactions with others, as teachers we have failed in helping our students to capture a true sense and understanding of servitude. Educators have a plethora of opportunities to cultivate and encourage these often tangled and sometimes conflicting dispositions. Simpson and his colleagues (Simpson, Jackson, and Aycock, 2005, 108) pose several questions that teachers should consider in terms of how educators can support the essence of service while engaging students in these important questions and conversations: How do we facilitate student interactions in regard to people choosing their own opinions and lifestyles and, at the same time, working toward the common good? When does open communication become a hindrance rather than a help to addressing differences of opinion? When, if ever, do we set aside personal aspirations for the good of society as a whole?

Defining service and developing a foundation for its importance within the educational community is critical to the art and profession of teaching. Defining and developing a sense of stewardship as an equal and complementary component to service is also an important aspect of a teacher's complete understanding of their impact on the educational community.

Stewardship

Stewardship in the educational community can be defined as the willingness to be accountable for the well-being of our constituents by operating in service, rather than in control, of those around us. In effect, stewardship is to hold something in trust for another. Historically, stewardship was a means to protect a kingdom while those rightfully in charge were away or, more often, to govern for the sake of an underage king (Block, 1993). The underage king, for educators, is the next generation. When we choose stewardship and service over self-interest, we build the capacity of the next generation (our students) to govern themselves.

Patriarchy versus Partnership

In a religious sense, a patriarch was one of the scriptural "fathers" of the human race or of the Hebrew people. It was often the oldest member of a representative group who members looked to as possessing wisdom and guidance. This also marked the supremacy of the male role and the legal dependence of wives and children, as well as the reckoning of descent and inheritance in the male bloodline. Of course, the counterpoint to this definition is a matriarchy where the representative group is led and/or "ruled" by the senior female member of the group.

Without getting into a long discussion of gender bias and comparisons within leadership roles, it is important to consider both patriarchy and matriarchy in the sense of a belief system that revolves around control of the environment and those within its structure. Control suggests that there is a clear line of authority, and from a traditional leadership style, a fundamental belief is that in order to organize effort toward a common goal, maintaining control, consistency, and predictability is a given. Decisions about rules, policy, and strategies are the domain of the leader at the top of the organizational pyramid, while people at the middle and the bottom exist to execute and implement these decisions.

The concepts of control, consistency, and predictability come from a behaviorist perspective, and on the surface, appear to be a commonsense and logical approach to governance. However, governance structures aimed at these three components work well in stable, predictable environments. School buildings and classrooms are not stable or predictable; a multitude of events and variables impact the environment on a daily basis. The patriarchal model, with power, reward, and privilege concentrated at the top, breeds self-interest and self-centeredness, which automatically creates an environment that lends itself to complaints about the patriarch.

Partnership and shared responsibility is perhaps the key component to stewardship in that it begins the process toward the establishment of balance of power and accountability. Partnership means to be connected to another in a way that the power between individuals is roughly balanced. Stewardship, the exercise of accountability as an act of service, requires a balance of power between parties to be credible (Block, 1993). An equal partnership requires not only a balance of power, but an opportunity to engage in dialogue to define a purpose. The traditional process has always been that management or upper-level senior individuals define the purpose and vision.

A true partnership means that each person in the organization takes on responsibility for defining these values, vision, and purpose. Purpose gets defined through dialogue and interaction. In the classroom environment, teachers should become stewards of this partnership in that they nourish a classroom and its students to allow for the creation of this balance of power. This does not take the authority or power of classroom "control" from the teacher, but allows for an understanding of balance in that a partnership does not always mean that you get what you want. It means you may lose the argument, but you never lose your voice and that you have the opportunity to express your opinions and thoughts. This kind of stewardship allows for the creation of a classroom environment where everyone contributes and everyone is encouraged to respect a variety of opinions.

The stewardship of this classroom partnership also involves joint celebration and accountability for growth, success, and failure. As servants and stewards to our students and the educational community, we are all accountable for academic success and we support each other in the oversight of behaviors that encourage an accepting classroom environment. The outcomes and quality of the classroom are everyone's responsibility, and everyone is accountable under the direction, guidance, and stewardship of the classroom teacher.

Patriarchal governance creates a social distance and vulnerability that encourages dishonesty from the fear of punishment or betrayal. One of the benefits of a redistribution of power and a successful partnership is that people feel less vulnerable (Block, 1993) and tend to be more open and honest about their goals and how they feel about the current environment. The stewardship of this partnership does not necessarily do away with hierarchy, and we still need leadership that includes specialized responsibility, but it is not in place so much for control as it is for clarity. In schools, teachers are still the content specialists, and building principals normally have specialized skills in school budgets, law, or curriculum issues.

There is nothing inconsistent between the encouragement of stewardship and partnership and being a boss. Stewardship remains as the willingness to hold power without using reward and punishment and oppressive or directive authority. Partnership is the willingness to give more choice to the people we choose to serve—not total control, just something closer to an equal balance of power. Stewardship maintains accountability for keeping things (the classroom) under control, but does not centralize the power or point of action. As soon as you centralize the point of action within the control of the teacher, you take away real ownership and responsibility from those closest to the work—the children that we teach and serve.

In the remaining chapters of this text, the focus turns to how teachers in the classroom can become servant leaders, specifically to their students, the parents, their colleagues and building administrators, and the local communities in which they serve.

CHAPTER FOUR

~

The Teacher as Servant Leader to Students

Sometimes you have to take with a grain of salt what your preceptor or college instructor is telling you, if that person is not emphasizing that your first obligation is to do what's in the best interest of children—not to please the administrators, not to raise test scores, not to keep order, not to carry out ludicrous legislative mandates. To help children become engaged and proficient thinkers and good people may require you to close your door, and it may require you to organize and subvert and rebel.

—Alfie Kohn

Alfie Kohn, author, writer, speaker, and educational social critic, emphasizes in his broad work—and specifically in his comment above—the need for effective teachers who are willing to sacrifice and make decisions that are in the best interest of students. We also know from a wealth of research that an effective teacher—more so than anything else—is the greatest predictor of student success. Effective teachers can influence and help students overcome many of the traditional social indicators usually blamed for student academic failure.

In his recent work, William Sanders has suggested that "ethnicity, poverty, and affluence can no longer be used as justifications for the failure [of students] to make academic progress. The single biggest factor affecting academic growth of any population of youngsters is the effectiveness of the individual classroom teacher. Furthermore, the teacher's effect on academic growth dwarfs and nearly renders trivial all these factors that people have historically worried about" (2003).

How we define effective teaching and our ability to identify characteristics that are indicators of an individual's capacity to impact the lives of students become the heart of our discussion. Although there are several good books on the market that suggest characteristics of successful, effective, and even extraordinary teachers, Richard Traina (1999), former president of Clark University, perhaps captured the essence of the characteristics of an effective teacher. After exploring the biographies and autobiographies of prominent nineteenth- and twentieth-century Americans, focusing on what they had to say about the traits of their most effective teachers, Traina recognized common themes that seem to reoccur in their stories.

First, the best teachers were remembered as being skillful and enthusiastic, having such a solid command of the subject matter that students could "pick up on their excitement" for the subject. Second, these teachers were caring—they cared deeply about each student and about that student's accomplishment and growth. Third, these teachers had distinctive character—there was a palpable energy that suffused the competent and caring teacher, some specific mark-making quality. In short, the effective and memorable teachers were skillful, enthusiastic, caring, and perhaps even idiosyncratic. Although the third trait, distinctive character, is elusive to define and perhaps impossible to teach, we can work to not destroy it by demanding conformity and narrow definitions of what successful teachers are (Digiulio, 2010).

Perhaps the distinctive character of an effective teacher is revealed as he or she teaches and interacts with students on a daily basis. If this is so, much of what we considered effective and distinctive teacher character qualities should revolve around efficacy—the teacher's belief that he or she will be successful because his or her students will also be successful.

As a servant leader to students, the effective teacher supports the needs of students in a variety of ways where the focus is on aspects of cognitive, psychological, and socioemotional growth. The age of the student is irrelevant in that to achieve student success (not necessarily defined by high test scores), extraordinary teachers serve students by helping them through three specific paths: producing, empowering, and connecting (Digiulio, 2010). By "producing," Digiulio suggests that student success is fostered by the work that students do, by what they produce rather than what we specifically do as teachers. By participating, performing, creating, practicing, designing, producing, experimenting, and engaging in a host of activities, what the student "does" will have a greater impact on how successful the student is (and feels) than what the teacher knows or says. By "empowering," Digiulio means actively teaching students how to help themselves, how to take responsibility for their work, how to get help, how to ask for help, whom to ask for help, and when to seek help. This is a real-world skill that starts in class, grows in school, and develops within the maturity of the child.

Students must be weaned from depending on their parents and teachers at every step. By "connecting," Digiulio hints at a Piagetian framework where success is fostered by student assignments and activities that connect yesterday, today, and tomorrow's information and learning. We all learn best when we learn that which is closest to what we already know. If we try to make sense of information that is alien to our experience or knowledge base, a disconnect naturally occurs. Making these cognitive connections is a core tenet of constructivism in which we construct our knowledge base relative to our experiences.

Certainly with the implementation of the No Child Left Behind Act, we want to guarantee that we have highly qualified teachers in every classroom, but we also want extraordinary, quality teachers in every classroom who not only have qualifying test scores and college degrees, but who also understand the importance of efficacy and caring, who understand how to empower and engage students, and who can maintain their own distinctive character that in fact helps to make them unique, creative, and inspiring teachers. As the goal of this chapter is to encourage the idea of the teacher as a servant leader to students, I now turn to a discussion of how teachers can become servants to their students, where serving not only supports academic success and cognitive skills but also supports the psychological and socioemotional growth and development of students in the classroom.

Serving Cognitive Development

Serving the cognitive development of students suggests setting the stage or providing the environment for learning to take place. Both Ralph Waldo Emerson and Henry Thoreau, as well as other writers, in a traditional sense envisioned the ultimate education and cognitive experience as one that does not simply pass on the end results of past cultural creations. A true cognitive experience immerses each student in the complete cycle of experiencing, formulating, and then reinstating these formulations back into experience to test, hone, and modify (The Thoreau Society, 1999). Take Emerson's comment that "only so much do I know, as I have lived. . . . So much only of life as I know by experience, so much of the wilderness have I vanquished and planted" (1983, 60), and Thoreau's vision in *Walden*, where he wrote, "Every man has to learn the points of the compass again as often as he wakes, whether from sleep or abstraction" (1971, 171) as he moved to and from Walden Pond. In each instance, both men suggested that learning is a perpetual journey, never completed and always a vibrant opportunity to build upon the immediate circumstances of life and experiences.

With Emerson, Thoreau, and even John Dewey, each of these philosophers saw learning—and, in fact, education—not simply as a means or preparation for something else but as an intrinsically valuable exercise. Each man saw a fundamental continuity between the schoolhouse door and the street, and between the process of learning and the rest of one's experience. Each also suggested that learning should go beyond the traditional dichotomy of teacher and student, suggesting that the teacher can also learn with and from the student. In essence, education should not simply transmit an existing culture of information but creatively reconstruct it (Bickman, 1999). Thoreau's insistence on "lived experience" as an essential element of education is the cornerstone of his and others' pedagogic beliefs.

In the spirit of Jean Piaget (1952), where cognition was seen as an interface between our senses and the real world, he and others (namely Neisser, 1976; Vygotsky, 1978; and Bruner, 1990) held in common at least three concepts or ideas that helped to explain the *process* of cognition and learning rather than the *product* of accumulated knowledge and information. First, they rejected empiricism (the belief that thought is a copy of reality) and innatism (the concept that ideas are inborn). Second, they did not believe that thought or cognition is built from simple associations in a passive process (in other words, learning takes active participation from the learner). And third, they believed that meaning is important and, therefore, context and active engagement are of critical importance.

We know from Piaget that the concepts of schema, assimilation, accommodation, and disequilibrium all play a significant role in learning and cognition and give us the opportunity to link yesterday's learning with today's experiences and tomorrow's new information. Disequilibrium is a part of the cognitive process in that we have to "suffer" cognitive imbalance to grow and learn. The successful resolution or regaining of cognitive equilibrium is where real learning takes place. We can, in effect, serve students cognitively by helping them to become better learners. Mindless classroom worksheets and word searches that are often considered "busy work" by students serve no purpose but to waste time, as little cognitive engagement is present. Challenging our students cognitively serves them in the long run by not only exercising their mental abilities, but also tapping into their creative and exploratory instincts.

Neil Postman and Charles Weingartner offer some fascinating insight in their text *Teaching as a Subversive Activity* (1969), where they offer several suggestions for developing and, in essence, serving students in a cognitive capacity. First, they suggest that teachers should tape to their mirror at home (or someplace where they will see this every day before they head off to school) the following questions: (1) What am I going to do today?, (2) What's it good for?, and (3) How do I know? At the least, teachers may begin to question why they teach things that have no specific value or where there is no evidence that specific anticipated outcomes actually occur. The questions may perhaps encourage you to reconsider everything you do. They may also encourage you to begin to critically assess the state or federally mandated standards, your textbooks, your syllabus, the grading system, your own education, administrative mandates, and other teaching habits that have become customary.

Second, Postman and Weingartner suggest trying to avoid telling your students any answers or solutions (if only for a few lessons or days). Pose to them some sort of problem without a prescribed lesson plan, and then allow them to work through potential solutions without your advice, input, or counsel. Your input is only generated by their comments and questions. Don't be frightened by long gaps of silence or hostile students. Silence might just mean your students are thinking about the situation, and apparent hostility might actually signify that students resent the idea that you have shifted the burden of intellectual activity and problem solving to them. This won't be an easy task in the beginning, but by incorporating this type of short activity on a daily or weekly basis, we can begin to serve students by helping them to be cognitive problem solvers rather than giving them answers.

Third, they suggest learning to listen to your students. Listening does not mean reacting to what they say. Therefore, any remark you offer is not designed to instruct or judge but rather is an attempt to clarify what was said. This activity takes time and patience on the part of the teacher, but it also allows for students to cognitively express themselves and to clarify their opinions and thoughts. Postman and Weingartner also suggest an effective classroom activity based on the work of therapist Carl Rogers that will also encourage students to become better active listeners. In this example, students engage in a discussion of some issue about which they have strong feelings. Their discussion can progress and a student can make any statement about the topic they like, but before they can speak, they must restate and summarize the previous speaker's opinion to the previous speaker's satisfaction. Often children (and adults) will find themselves concentrating on what others are saying to the point that they become enthusiastic listeners, with the principle outcome of becoming a better listener and actually understanding what others perceive as relevant. As a result, we all become better listeners, and perhaps teachers will become better servants by designing more effective lessons based on what students actually know, feel, and care about.

Fourth, Postman and Weingartner recommend assisting your students to formulate thoughtful questions about important topics. At first, don't worry about the quality of questions; have students brainstorm a quantity of questions just to have the opportunity to examine these more in depth and to determine at a later date certain criteria that make a quality question. This later criteria might include: (1) Does the question contain certain invalid assumptions?, (2) Does it leave important terms undefined?, and (3) Does it suggest a procedure or protocol for obtaining an answer? Depending on the age of your students, the following are some potential problem-solving topics that would generate lots of questions:

1. If we wanted to make our school a "better" school, what would we need to know in order to proceed?
2. We have lots of trash around our school. What could we do to eliminate this and improve the "look" of our school?
3. Suppose our job is to make recommendations to improve the bus traffic flow at our school at specific drop-off points. What would you need to know to suggest a solution?

Finally, they recommend having students pose futuristic questions with futuristic responses. If you have noticed, most examinations focus on past knowledge—students provide us with established knowledge about subjects and information. Future-oriented questions can serve cognitively to motivate students (since there is not a right or wrong answer) and to allow students to be creative without the hazards or fear of grades or punishment for incorrect answers. Our society is a rapidly changing, future-oriented world, and by the time many of these students have finished school, the future you have asked them to think about will be the present (Postman and Weingartner, 1969). Depending on the age level of your students, possible questions may be something like this:

Based upon new technological inventions, what impact will the following have on our future society?

a. Cars that can be powered by water?
b. Disposable "paper" clothing?

c. Complete nutritious meals in the form of a pill?
d. Interplanetary communication?
e. The ability to clone and "grow" multiple body organs (heart, lungs, kidneys, etc.)?

In the end, serving the cognitive needs of children is dependent on the teacher's own creativity and ability to work within the current educational system while thinking outside of the proverbial standardization box. As Thoreau stated:

> I left the woods for as good a reason as I went there. Perhaps it seemed to me that I had several more lives to live and could not spare any more time for that one. It is remarkable how easily and insensibly we fall into a particular route, and make a beaten track for ourselves. I had not lived there a week before my feet wore a path from my door to the pond-side; and though it is five or six years since I have trod it, it is still quite distinct. It is true, I fear that others may have fallen into it, and so helped to keep it open. The surface of the earth is soft and impressible by the feet of men; and so with the paths which the mind travels. How worn and dusty, then, must be the highways of the world, how deep the ruts of tradition and conformity. (1971, 323)

Serving our students cognitively requires that we encourage them to step off the well-worn path at times without fear of becoming lost or scrutinized for their curiosity and willingness to explore.

Serving Psychological Development

Every teacher should have a solid grasp of their assumptions about teaching and learning and how their assumptions translate into a positive learning environment in their classroom. Mandates from the federal government or state departments of education are often attached to a political agenda that centers on raising test scores and holding teachers and school administrators accountable for what is superficially defined as "learning." Every teacher has a professional responsibility to analyze and explore every new mandate and standard in terms of its educational validity and to what extent these new "rules" support the learning of children.

Without thinking teachers who can critically assess new rules and mandates, we do not have thinking schools. Without thinking schools, we do not have thinking students or future citizens who can think. Teachers who are timid and automatically follow and obey mandates without question while never stopping to consider the pros and cons or political agendas attached to these mandates are dangerous (Page, 2010). This timidity often undermines the courage that it takes to be a successful teacher and a servant to students.

> The courage you need is the courage to not excuse yourself too often for failing to do what needs doing, for pretending that bad practice—including your own—is good practice, or for seeing yourself and your colleagues as the enemy—or the victims. Victims don't make good teachers—because above all we want our kids to see themselves as competent actors who have learned how to be competent citizens from teachers who saw themselves as that—citizens of their schools and communities. (Meier, 2010, 216)

Serving students in a competent cognitive fashion helps set the stage for active learning and for future academic success. Serving students' psychological development is equally important in that psychological well-being provides a mentally safe environment for students to reach their full potential.

Before discussing issues of psychological development, it is important to define several key concepts that are often misunderstood or misinterpreted. Self-esteem, also referred to as self-worth or self-image, is the global evaluative dimension of the self. For example, an adolescent or emerging adult might perceive themselves as not merely a person, but a good person. The concept of self-esteem refers to one's global self-evaluation. Self-concept refers to domain-specific evaluations of the self. Examples could be academic and athletic abilities or an individual's perception of their physical appearance. Self-concept, then, refers to specific domain-related self-evaluation. Self-efficacy refers to a belief that one can master a situation or concept and produce favorable outcomes; self-efficacy is the belief that "I can," whereas helplessness is the belief that "I cannot."

When students begin to think of "how well" they are doing as opposed to "what they are doing," Kohn (1999a, 28) and a host of other researchers begin to suggest the following academic and potential psychological outcomes. First, when students (and their teachers and parents) primarily focus on "how well" they are doing, it typically undermines the students' interest in learning. Second, it typically makes failure seem overwhelming when constant comparisons are made to those who seem to be doing well. Third, when "how well" you are doing is the constant focus, students will begin to avoid challenges in fear of failure. Fourth, this constant focus reduces the quality of learning, as we emphasize learning at a set standardized level. Fifth, the emphasis on "how well" we are learning encourages students to think about how smart they are rather than their effort or how hard they may have tried to accomplish a task (Kohn, 1999a).

A combination of several motivational researchers, theorists, and critics has further defined several of the psychological components that not only impact student motivation, but also set the tone for future learning and appropriate goal setting. Carol Dweck (1986) suggested that there are two types of goal orientations—performance goals and learning goals—each of which dramatically impacts motivation. If we have performance goals, the process of comparing our abilities to others or a specific norm or of completing specific tasks to please others becomes paramount. Performance goals may well create conditions or an internal attitude that in fact undermines intrinsic motivation. When so much emphasis is placed on good grades or high test scores, the process and enjoyment of learning and exploring new information becomes secondary to how we perceive ourselves compared to other students.

Students with learning goal orientations focus on the task and pleasure of learning and are willing to engage in more difficult activities, since for them, a comparison to other students is not important. This also suggests that student reactions to failure may vary greatly depending on what type of goal orientation they have. With performance goals, failure is seen as a reflection of their innate abilities and their failure to compete with others on a specific task. In contrast, students with learning goal orientations tend to have a healthy, resilient attitude toward failure and appear to see failure as part of the learning process. Their attitude is generally more positive when they are not successful, and they think of ways to be more successful that might include the development of new strategies and an increase in effort and hard work. Students with performance goals have a positive attitude as long as they are successful. But when problems arise and they see themselves as less capable when compared to other students, they react as helpless or regard themselves as failures. These students are always potentially vulnerable to failure and the psychological experience it brings. When the point isn't to figure things out but to prove how good you are, it's often hard to cope with being told you're not so good (Kohn, 1999b).

A second component of goal orientation is the issue of how we accept challenging activities. If the point is specifically to succeed, wherein we measure our success by a predetermined benchmark or we compare ourselves to others' success, we might typically choose the easiest task that can be completed in the shortest amount of time. This decision will maximize the probability of success, minimize the probability of failure, and make us feel psychologically good, knowing that we did as well as anyone else. Students with strong learning goals typically choose more difficult tasks that are interesting to them since they don't worry about failure. If our students' focus can remain on the opportunity to learn and the intrinsic value of the task, rather than how well they do a task compared to others, learning goals can work toward the pursuit of more challenging and creative work.

Attribution theory also plays a role in psychological health and particularly our motivation toward future goals and challenges. As Bernard Weiner (1979) suggested in his groundbreaking work, how we attribute our success and failure at a difficult task will ultimately impact how we approach the next task. If we make 100 percent on our exam and attribute this success to outside influences (the teacher was easy, I got lucky, etc.), we most likely will not have the confidence to think that we might get lucky again or that the next test will also be easy, so we attribute this success to outside forces over which we have no control. By the same token, if we attribute our success to our hard work, effort, study time, etc., we have attributed our success to factors that we control. We can increase our effort or study time or even change the method of how we study material, but we can't control the difficulty of the test or our chances to get lucky.

By the same token, if I receive a failing grade on a test and I attribute this to my poor intelligence or a harsh teacher, again these are factors that are not under my control. However, if I fail a test and attribute this to my lack of studying or reading material to prepare, these are factors that are within my power to manipulate and change. So the key is to understand that when children are encouraged to focus on how well they are performing in school, they tend to explain their performance not by how hard they tried but by how smart they are (Kohn, 1999b). When performance-oriented students ask the questions of: How am I doing? Am I improving fast enough? Are my grades high enough? Did I pass the state mandated exam? Am I doing better than the person sitting next to me?—each is likely to focus on what they perceive as their ability and intelligence.

If children are poor readers, we don't want them to attribute their failure to lack of ability, since ability is linked to intelligence and we think of intelligence as unchangeable. With this perception, there is no hope for a more positive outcome in the future. In a sense, we have helped to create a child who will become helpless. If they attribute their failure to lack of effort, hard work, or poor study skills, these can all be changed and improved upon, therefore setting the stage for a more optimistic outlook toward the next task. When we focus so much on results (test scores), we often forget about the process or activity that produced those results.

Serving Socioemotional Growth

In many ways, teaching and learning are about the development of interpersonal and intrapersonal relationships. Interpersonal relationships are relationships (associations, interactions, and communication) with others, or more specifically, between two or more people. Intrapersonal relationships are how individuals relate, reflect, monitor, and understand themselves. Part of building a supportive learning environment and, in fact, serving the needs of students rests with the interactions of the teacher and their students, colleagues, administrators, parents, and families. It is vital to psychological health to also understand and support the emotional growth of students and to promote positive relationships among students in the classroom.

For the purposes of this discussion, serving the socioemotional growth of children means encouraging the interrelationships of children within the classroom or school environment, and helping students to understand and reflect on their own goals and future pursuits. Embedded within the development of emotional support in the social atmosphere of the classroom or school is the distinction between two models of growth, one being a "demand" model and the other being a "support" (in essence, a service) model. Eric Schaps, director of the Developmental Studies Center in Oakland, California, has suggested a single distinction between focusing on what students ought to be able to do—basically, what we demand of them—in contrast to what we can do to support students' development and learning (Kohn, 1994).

The demand model encourages a coercion of students to achieve at a certain level or to work toward specific outcomes that are predetermined by federal, state, or district standards. With this model, the specific outcome or level of achievement is key, and responsibility and consideration of the curriculum and the context in which learning takes place is ignored. Since the level of expected student achievement is preset by outside forces, all students are expected to achieve at this level, regardless of family history, circumstances, or cognitive capacity. The context of socioeconomic status, parental support, student mobility from one school to another, ethnic and gender differences, and unique family issues are ignored since the achievement goal and expectations are predetermined before the child enters the classroom.

In contrast, a support or service model encourages teachers to focus on guiding and stimulating children's natural inclination to explore the unfamiliar, to construct meaning, and to develop a competence with a passion for playing with words, numbers, and ideas (Kohn, 1994). Nicholls and Hazzard (1993) have even suggested that this supportive service model helps children take part in an "adventure in ideas." Rather than the classroom being "teacher-centered," positive learning environments must be "student- or learner-centered," where the focus is to serve students to assist them to make sense of their world. As Kohn (1994) has stated, improvement is not something that is required, but more so something that follows when we provide students with engaging tasks and a supportive environment without the overbearing demand of meeting a specific standard with a certain competency.

Of course, all of this discussion is influenced and perhaps dependent upon how we define achievement or success in our classrooms, and ultimately how we measure the accomplishments of our students. With the demand model, assessments are predetermined and levels of accomplishments are standardized at minimum competencies for all children, regardless of context or background. With a support and service model, assessment and student support is interpreted quite differently; therefore, the teacher, classroom, and school environment take on a different climate structure that becomes void of the psychological aspects of potential failure or peer comparisons. Kohn (1994) has suggested five principles of assessment that can be supported from a support and service model.

First, assessment of any kind should not be overdone. The current obsession with testing and assessment begins to undermine students' creative interests, particularly with the preoccupation with the mandates of federal and state officials. Remember, as a part of motivational theory, performance-based orientations can actually result in students avoiding difficult tasks so that they can avoid either a negative evaluation or failure. An excessive concern with performance begins to erode curiosity and subsequently begins to eliminate motivation toward exploring anything new or interesting.

Second, the best evidence we have of whether teachers are succeeding as educators comes from observing children's behavior (in a qualitative sense), rather than from test scores or grades (a quantitative measure). When we observe and see students discussing and perhaps arguing animatedly about an issue or concept raised in class after the class is over, or when children arrive home chattering about what was learned at school that day, or when they read more about a topic they have suddenly become interested in, in each case, an interest has been sparked and new skills are usually acquired. As Kohn has suggested, interest is difficult to quantify, but the solution is not to return to more conventional measuring methods; it is to acknowledge the potential limits of quantitative measurement.

Third, schools and classrooms must be transformed into safe, caring communities. If the classroom becomes a safe place where there is no fear of humiliation and punitive judgment, it begins to create an environment where students can become good learners, good people, and creative explorers of new information. When the classroom, school, and district climate places such a high emphasis on grades, standardization, testing, and reaching mandatory skills, teachers and students become more automated and the curriculum more prescribed to the point that it makes assessing students on an individual basis much more difficult.

Fourth, conversations about testing and assessment must also include conversations about the quality of curriculum. The most important question to ask in this situation is, have the students been given anything that is worth learning? Research results have suggested that when students are given interesting and exciting things to do and explore, external or artificial inducements to boost achievement become unnecessary (Moeller and Reschke, 1993). An important question then becomes, does the curriculum drive the need for assessment, or does the need for assessment drive the curriculum?

Fifth, students should play a role in determining the criteria by which their work is judged and then play a role in weighing their work against the criteria. In today's educational world, we almost never involve students in decisions of curriculum, criteria, and assessment. Kohn (1993) has suggested that students should make decisions about as many elements of their learning as possible. By allowing them some of this decision-making power, it gives them more control over their education, makes evaluation less punitive, and provides an important learning experience by engaging students in the decision-making process.

In each of the recommendations listed above by Kohn, ultimately we set the stage for students to become more learning goal oriented rather than performance goal oriented, and we encourage students to attribute their successes (and sometimes failures) to characteristics or attributes that are within their realm to control, namely their hard work, effort, perseverance, self-regulation, and specific interests and curiosity. More important than obtaining or meeting specific standards, we need to serve students by helping them to acquire the habits of mind to become good human beings—good parents, good friends, and good citizens of our democracy. We need to serve our students by helping them to learn to care about themselves, to care about one another, and to care also about people they've never met (Ohanian, 1999).

Serving and supporting students in the near future will not become an easier task. If we are not careful, teachers will find themselves serving legislative mandates, or state standards created by those far removed from the classroom. Standardized, state-mandated exams, along with No Child Left Behind legislative regulations and the demand that schools make annual yearly progress (AYP), only serve to automatize students' learning toward specific tasks. Serving the cognitive, psychological, and socioemotional needs of students and creating classrooms that can support this effort cannot be accomplished by using an industrial or business model. Children are not products on an assembly line that can be mass-produced in quantities according to precise or standardized specifications. Each child is unique, with a unique background and unique previous learning experiences.

As Susan Ohanian (1999) eloquently states, Thoreau's *Walden* isn't really about the woods and Edward Abbey's *Desert Solitaire* isn't about the desert. What those books are really about are living alone, living with purpose, and living with honor. In a deeper sense, standardized exams and federal and state mandates are not about curriculum and helping students to become better learners; they are about bureaucracy, group-think, and controlling other people. Serving students requires teachers to reflect and to understand who you are, where you are, and liking what you find. Being a servant teacher to your students means being able to find your own way and charting your own path, rather than relying on standardized curriculum, standards, and automated instruction. Allowing students to experience the creative energy of learning in which they control the creative juices and outcomes of their exploration is a difficult task, but not without merit and satisfaction for both the teacher and student.

As she closes her text *One Size Fits Few* (1999, 152), Ohanian again states what are classic words of advice for the teacher who would be a servant leader: "To be a teacher, you've got to stop your frantic busyness, stop what you're doing, stop looking for what you're looking for, stop expecting what you're expecting, stop promising to deliver the [state or federal standards] product on schedule. Stop, and just be there for the child—for however long it takes. Stop is a good word for teachers. It is a very good word for a teacher to take to heart. Stop."

We know from good research that excellent teachers can make the difference in the academic success of students in the classroom. However, teachers are there to serve not only their students' cognitive development and learning, but also their psychological and emotional well-being. Students need to see in us, their teachers, a strong work ethic, character, self-discipline, self-regulation, self-confidence without arrogance, and our passionate desire to serve their needs, whatever those needs might be at the moment.

As servant leaders in the teaching profession, we serve the needs of the children we teach while also understanding and serving, in a limited sense, the needs of their parents and families. Serving the parents and families of our students is the focus of our next chapter.

~

CHAPTER FIVE

The Teacher as Servant Leader to Parents and Families

To educate children without a deep partnership of teacher and parent is hopeless.

—Patrick Dolan

Parents and families help set the stage for students to develop the capacity for self-control, persistence, and learning patience and respect for others (Eberly, 1995). When children are treated with respect and as worthwhile human beings by their families, and when parents model care and concern, children also learn these attributes and school personnel are able to develop classroom atmospheres and learning environments that facilitate these characteristics as well as learning (McCall, 1995). Schools also have a great desire to help children acquire skills in working with their peers and gaining the ability to interact with adults in appropriate interaction and dialogue. Children who seem to be able to acquire skills like following directions, completing tasks, getting along with others, taking turns, and recognizing the rights of others also seem to excel academically. By default, families that encourage these traits, along with instilling the value of education and helping children to approach and complete difficult tasks, are setting the stage for a positive school experience (Goldstein, 1995).

Parent and family interest and support is critical for student success. Parents' interest has many beneficial effects for children, but the benefit is particularly great for children from single-parent families, a group that is normally at greater risk of school failure than those with two-parent homes

(Zill, 1996). The research is clear on the positive impact that families and parents can have on the educational success of their children. Therefore, the key for teachers is to determine how we can encourage these key players to become involved in their children's education and how we as teachers can become servant leaders to these parents and families that are so critical to their children's success in school.

Responsiveness

In most organizational structures, employees devote a great deal of their time and energy to listening to their customers. Although I don't like to use an industrial or corporate model analogy when discussing schools and education since children are not duplicate assembly line products, listening to "customers" helps organizational members to learn what their customers regard as strengths and weaknesses. Listening also helps members to understand what is being done well and what needs to be improved. Teachers who strive to be servant leaders are much like the organizational employees in that the more responsive and better listeners they become, the more actively they can serve parents and families at their level.

Responsive schools and teachers hold themselves accountable first and foremost to the people who depend on the school's performance—parents, students, and the community—and serve these entities to their greatest capacity (Seyfarth, 1999). Servant teachers take on this responsibility of promoting children's welfare, a duty that takes precedence over everything else. By definition, responsive teachers who are also servant leaders are adaptable and listen to the needs of parents. Simple efforts that include having a helpful and friendly front office staff, returning parent phone calls and e-mails, and communicating when there are good things to report about students rather than just when there's poor behavior are all given indicators of responsiveness that don't require much time or effort but indicate a concentrated commitment to serving parents.

Recent research also indicates the positive impact of home visits by teachers and administrators before school begins and during the school year, making the effort to meet parents in a setting that is psychologically and physically convenient and comfortable for them while encouraging them to be active participants in their children's education and, eventually, the school setting (Acosta, Keith, and Patin, 1997). Home visits help teachers to understand the needs of parents in the context of the family setting and send a clear message that teachers care about their specific child and his or her growth and development. This type of service forces teachers to explore outside their comfort zones and to actually see the environment, setting, and family interactions of their students' daily lives. Responsiveness means meeting the needs of parents and families and understanding how you can provide and assist them to be even more supportive and engaged in their child's educational experience.

Increasing Parent Involvement

The research is clear suggesting that parent involvement in schools is highly correlated with school and teacher satisfaction and the academic success of children. Anytime we can encourage parents and families to read to children, assist with homework, contact teachers with concerns, assist as volunteers at school, attend school functions, and take an active part in school decisions and governance, both parties potentially win from the experiences. Parents benefit by gaining more information about the school and what they can do to be supportive of their children, and teachers learn more about the lives of the children they teach, which helps them to be more effective teachers (Davies, 1993).

If we know that parent involvement in their children's education and school is critical for success, why, then, do schools struggle with parents taking an active part in their children's schooling? Although parents are busy with jobs and are often involved in time scheduling conflicts that limit more active participation in schools, research does suggest that an overwhelming number of parents report that they help their children with homework when teachers ask them to and that they would even offer more assistance if they had specific directions on how to help. This finding indicates that most parents want to see their children do well in school. Time constraints and organizational patterns of how schools are designed are at times prohibitive of parent involvement. The typical trend is that many parents are intimately involved in schools when their children are at the elementary level and become less involved as children progress through middle and high school settings.

Most elementary schools are smaller and provide a less intimidating atmosphere, and elementary school structures include perhaps one or two teachers that are immediate contacts for parents while secondary settings are larger and offer a less intimate setting, with perhaps four, five, or more teachers and coaches as contact points. School contacts in regard to parent-teacher conference days and school event scheduling often only add to the frustration of parents when these times are scheduled during the normal workday, when parents are not as available.

Although elementary teachers want their students to become independent thinkers and learners, part of the elementary experience is designed to teach and help students learn these skills and attributes. Middle school and high school teachers expect students to be more independent and responsible for their own learning and are often less likely to contact parents when students encounter problems, both behavioral and academic (Eccles and Harold, 1996). Certainly at the secondary level, teachers can serve parents and families more closely by contacting parents more often in regard to concerns that may arise in the classroom. Another issue to consider is that at the elementary level, parents feel more competent to assist and ask questions about the work their students are engaged in, whereas secondary content becomes more specific and advanced. Many parents feel less capable of assisting their children academically and are often more concerned with their own limitations and abilities. This outcome begins to suggest that parent and family involvement is related to feelings of efficacy in communicating with school personnel.

Conferences with caregivers and parents are often expected of elementary school teachers and can be just as important in middle and high school. The more skilled teachers are at communicating, the more effective they will be at conducting these conferences. When you are working with parents and families that are angry or upset, make sure you really hear the concerns of the participants, not just their words. Use reflection to clarify. The atmosphere should be friendly and unrushed and should always have the best interests of the child at the forefront. Conversations about the child should be factual, based on observation. Educators and researchers increasingly recognize how important it is for teachers and parents to jointly guide the learning of children, especially those with specific disabilities (Friend, 2006; Hallahan and Kauffman, 2006).

Parent involvement is the number one priority in improving education (Chira, 1993). If both parents are involved in their child's schooling, students are more likely to excel and less likely to repeat a grade or be expelled (National Center for Educational Statistics, 1997; Epstein, 2001, 2005, 2007a, 2007b; Epstein and Sheldon, 2006). Families have the basic obligation to provide for the safety and health of their children. However, schools can provide family programs that help parents understand age-appropriate changes and can provide information about health, sexually transmitted diseases, depression, drugs, and alcohol. Schools can also provide or help parents find safe places for their adolescent to spend time away from home. Schools and teachers have a basic obligation to communicate with families about school programs and the individual progress of their children, with the intent to inform and to increase parent involvement in schools.

Student-led conferences—in essence, parent-teacher-student-led conferences (Popham, 1995; Stiggins, 2001)—have also been shown to effectively support parent involvement. With student-led conferences, we increase the likelihood of parent participation, encourage students to reflect on their own academic progress and behavior, and give students practice in leadership and communication skills. Students whose parents are involved have better attendance records, higher achievement, and more positive attitudes toward learning, while parents gain a better idea of how to help their children (Davis and Thomas, 1989; Epstein, 1996; Levin and Lezotte, 1995; Hill and Craft, 2003; Mattingly, Prislin, McKenzie, Rodrigues, and Kayzar, 2002). Most parents will become involved in school only when they have a specific invitation to do so and when they know that the school genuinely wants them to be involved (Carr, 1997; Hoover-Dempsey and Sandler, 1997).

Ormrod (2010) has provided several suggestions for getting reluctant parents to become more involved in schools. Teachers should make an extra effort to gain parents' trust and confidence by convincing them that you value their input. Encourage parents to be assertive when they have questions or concerns. Invite other important family members to the school (e.g. grandparents) to participate in activities. Give parents suggestions for learning activities they can easily do with their children at home. Find out what parents do exceptionally well and ask them to share. Provide opportunities for parents to volunteer for jobs that they can do at home. Identify specific individuals who can translate. Conduct parent-teacher conferences at times and locations more convenient for families. Make use of home visits if they are welcome.

Some parents have a strong sense of self-efficacy and have the skill and confidence to take actions that ensure they will have a voice in decisions that involve their children. Other parents lack this confidence and ability. Therefore, it becomes important to understand this lack of confidence and hesitancy and to serve parents in ways that help them to gain this ability. Assisting them to understand the culture and process of schools and to feel more capable in asking questions and engaging in the appropriate pursuit of answers becomes an important skill.

Parent Partnerships

Partnerships between schools and parents tend to be built through communication, and schools and teachers that hope to develop strong partnerships with parents must effectively communicate this desire. Part of serving parents and families is the ability to communicate effectively and to nurture these partnerships with a genuine desire to improve the school climate. In developing effective parent and family partnerships, communication must be a two-way interaction from the school to home and from the home to school (Seyfarth, 1999).

The beginning of effective partnerships involves the dissemination of information in a variety of ways that includes newsletters with information about budgets, curriculum, student achievement and performance, as well as upcoming school and community events. In today's world, using simple technology that includes voice mail, e-mail, and school Web site announcements is a necessity, but many low-income families and students for whom English is not the central language in the home have more difficulties with electronic communication access. Nurturing partnerships for all parents and families requires multiple language abilities at times and direct communication.

Parents play important roles in children's success in schools. Among the ways that parents can positively contribute to children's school success is through effective family management practices and being involved in their children's schooling. Researchers have found that family management practices are positively related to grades and self-responsibility, and negatively related to school-related problems. Among the family management practices important in this regard are maintaining structured, organized routines like homework, chores, and consistent bedtime routines. Creating a family environment in which high expectations for achievement are present is also important. Although teachers may not have the immediate or direct ability to impact family structures and expectations in the home, they can serve as a resource to encourage these kinds of good habits with improved communication.

The ability to communicate directly and in person has its advantages, and these skills are highly prized by school counselors, administrators, and teachers. E-mail access and accounts, social networking sites, and, in today's world, Twitter pages are effective communication resources in their own right, but they do have their limitations. In terms of recognizing body language, emotions, and communication pauses and contextual phrases, electronic forms of communication cannot always convey the correct message and cannot always convey a passion, honesty, or sincerity that is so critical in building relationships. Direct communication involves speaking honestly with parents about issues that concern them the most, and in a format and setting that will provide them with confidence. Developing this type of communication will result in more partnerships and more effective relationships with parents in support of their children.

Serving parents, effectively communicating, and developing partnerships involve providing parents with your time and also resources that can be useful for them to understand schools and their child's progress. The better teachers are able to anticipate questions and prepare for these conversations, the more effectively these relationships will begin to develop. Parents want to know how their child is taught and what they are learning. They want to know about placement decisions and how their child is progressing in regard to their age and grade-appropriate level. They want to know what their child is expected to learn and how they can help their child do better in school academically and in their relationships with other teachers, staff, and peers. They may need report cards and standardized test scores interpreted so that they can understand if their child is effectively progressing.

Support of the child should always be a partnership where both parents and teachers are engaged, where both parents and teachers are communicating often, and where both parents and teachers are making decisions that are in the best interest of the behavioral, social, and academic development of the child. Teachers who are servant leaders anticipate this interaction, lead these conversations in this direction, and provide parents and families with a sense of partnership and support.

Service to Diverse Populations and Those with Limited English Skills

Public schools in the United States for many years have taken a position of focusing their efforts toward middle-income to high-income students and directing their communication efforts toward the English-speaking, white majority student population. Today, it is no longer unusual for a school to have multiple languages spoken in one school setting, and in some instances, twenty to thirty—or more—languages or dialect variations may be heard in some diverse urban school settings. Meetings with students and parents are moving toward those with simultaneous translations in English, Spanish, Vietnamese, Burmese, and various Chinese dialects (Davis, 1995). In such school and community settings, being responsive teacher servants requires finding ways to reach families whose language and culture are different from the majority of school personnel. Being responsive also may require that we find ways to reach families and parents with options other than traditional outreach programs. Often, these immigrant families or those with limited English skills may not be as involved in the school, not only due to their lack of language skills but also due to the difference in their cultural attitudes about the role parents should play in their children's education and development.

Culture is the behaviors and belief systems that characterize a long-standing social group. One's cultural background influences the perspectives and values one acquires, the skills one masters and finds important, and the adult roles to which one aspires. It also guides the development of language skills, expression, and regulation of emotions, and the formation of a sense of self (Ormrod, 2010). We can also see considerable variation in attitudes and behaviors within a particular culture; individuals may adopt some cultural values and practices but reject others (Tudge, Hogan, Lee, Tammeveski, Meltsas, Kulakova, Snezhkova, and Putnam, 1999).

An ethnic group is a group of individuals with a common culture and common characteristics. Its roots either precede the creation of or are external to the country in which the group resides; for example, it may be comprised of people of the same race, national origin, or religious background. Its members share a sense of interdependence—a sense that their lives are intertwined (NCSS Task Force on Ethnic Studies Curriculum Guidelines, 1992). You can't determine students' ethnicity strictly based on physical characteristics (e.g. race) or birthplace (Wlodkowski and Ginsberg, 1995). Many students enter school for the first time and experience culture shock (Casanova, 1987; Ramsey, 1987). Although most schools in North America are based on Western European American, middle-class, "mainstream culture," students who are recent immigrants may not know these different norms regarding acceptable behavior, and they may find schools confusing and incomprehensible.

Recent immigrants may not know what to expect from others or what behaviors others expect from them (Harris, 1991; Igoa, 1995). Children, raised in a society where gender roles are clearly differentiated and where males and females are expected to behave differently, may have difficulty adjusting to school (Kirschenbaum, 1989; Vasquez, 1988). This culture mismatch between home and school may interfere with students' adjustment to the school setting and ultimately with their academic achievement (Garcia, 1995; Lee and Slaughter-Defoe, 1995; Ogbu, 1992).

Like many parents in the United States, most foreign-born parents value education, but many are not as likely to expect to have an active voice in decisions about their children's schooling. Decisions about how to spend school funds, school conduct codes, and school curriculum and standards are perhaps not left up to parents in their home countries, and these foreign-born parents may be surprised to be asked for their input (Valdes, 1996). In their culture, these types of decisions are left up to school authorities, with little input from parents.

New immigrant parents may attend school functions when invited, but they may not actively seek information about their child's school performance and may not understand how to ask for assistance to help their child do better in school. Many may also hesitate to speak to administrators or teachers due to the language barrier, and may also fear that they may say something wrong that would make life more difficult for their child (Valdes, 1996). In some cultures, teachers are highly respected, and parents are fearful that teachers will think that they are not confident in the abilities or decision-making ability of the teachers. They may often avoid asking questions even though their children might benefit from the information they might gain from the interaction (Yao, 1993).

These types of cultural differences may also place students and their parents at odds with one another. This cultural disparity of students becoming more "Americanized" while their parents hold fast to their home culture's traditional values often places the teacher in a position of a supportive mediator. Many cultural values differ from those in a traditional Western system, and while we may think activities like dating, driving a car, and participating in athletic and other extracurricular activities are the developmental norm, for many in non-Western countries, these activities are not welcomed and, in fact, strongly discouraged (Yao, 1993).

In other cases, some immigrant cultures do not envision moving on through an extensive educational system, and adequate educations are defined as fourth- or fifth-grade equivalencies. They may also expect their children to forego "selfish" wants or desires to help with family needs, which may mean that students are encouraged to drop out of school and go to work to help support the family economically (Valdes, 1996).

In the United States, more than six million students speak a language other than English at home, and in some large city school systems, more than one hundred different languages are spoken (McKeon, 1994; National Association of Bilingual Education, 1993; U.S. Bureau of the Census, 1994). Students who have not encountered English before will naturally have difficulty with schoolwork and classroom assessments in English-based classrooms. When a local dialect is the language most preferred by residents of a community, it is often the means through which people can most effectively connect with one another on a day-to-day basis. Many children, adolescents, and their parents view their native dialect as an integral part of their ethnic identity (Garrison, 1989; McAlpine, 1992; Ogbu, 1999). Ideally, children and adolescents from diverse backgrounds probably function most effectively when they use both their local dialect and standard English in appropriate settings (Gollnick and Chinn, 2002; Ogbu, 1999; Warren and McCloskey, 1993).

Western culture engages in an abundance of communication and discourse, sometimes without much to say (Trawick-Smith, 2003). In other cultures, silence is golden (Menyuk and Menyuk, 1988). Within specific groups, talking a lot can be interpreted as a sign of immaturity or low intelligence (Minami and McCabe, 1996). Different groups also have different ideas about when it's appropriate for children to speak or to ask questions (Garcia, 1994; Gutierrez and Rogoff, 2003). Some would suggest that children who speak directly and assertively to adults are rude and perhaps rebellious (Delgado-Gaitan, 1994; Lomawaima, 1995). A child who looks an adult in the eye is often interpreted as showing disrespect (Irujo, 1988; Torres-Guzman, 1998). Some cultures stand physically close together when they talk (Sue, 1990; Slonim, 1991), while others need much more personal space, especially when they don't know each other very well (Trawick-Smith, 2003).

Question-and-answer sessions like the traditional IRE cycle (Teacher [I] initiates an interaction, student [R] responds, teacher [E] evaluates) (Mehan, 1979) may also create anxiety, as some cultures are not comfortable with questioning (Losey, 1995; Rogoff, 2003; Crago, Annahatak, and Ningiuruvik, 1993). At times, children may have little experience with certain kinds of questions. Some parents in the southeastern United States may ask questions that involve comparisons and analogies. Rather than saying, "What's that?" they may ask, "What's that like?" (Heath, 1989). Sometimes students are taught not to answer some types of personal questions from strangers (Heath, 1980), and in some settings, lengthy pauses in response to questions are more important and considered appropriate and respectful (Gilliland, 1988). When given more time to respond, students from such cultures are more likely to participate in class and answer questions (Grant and Gomez, 2001). Some may interrupt spontaneously and simultaneously; if you wait, you may be excluded from the conversation (Slonim, 1991; Tharp, 1989).

When teachers ask students to demonstrate skills in public, it may confuse or alienate students (Garcia, 1994; Lomawaima, 1995). Some are more comfortable responding as a group (Miller, 1995). Students from some cultures are not comfortable in competitive situations (Garcia, 1992; Lomawaima, 1995). Students feel responsible for their families' well-being, and a strong sense of loyalty to other family members may influence them to leave school to help at home (Timm and Borman, 1997). In most cultures, traditional school academic achievement is highly valued (Duran and Weffer, 1992;

Goldenburg, Gallimore, Reese, and Garnier, 2001; Yee, 1992), while in some cultures, non-traditional academics (art, music, dance) are more highly valued than subjects like reading and math (Kirschenbaum, 1989; Reed, 1989). When teachers understand these cultural differences and when parents realize that educators want students to succeed in the classroom, they are more apt to work cooperatively to promote student achievement (Banks and Banks, 1995; Salend and Taylor, 1993).

An emphasis on punctuality for some Hispanic and Native American cultures is a struggle, since many do not adhere to strict schedules and timelines (Gilliland, 1988). As servants to parents, we must be sensitive to the ways in which students of various cultures and ethnic groups are likely to think and act differently from one another and help students to also develop this sensitivity. Like the fish that is unaware of water until it has left the water, people often take their own community's ways of doing things for granted (Rogoff, 2003, 13). We assume that good parents control their children, and these kinds of ways of thinking are often so pervasive in our lives, we expect this to be good behavior. In a sense, these types of ways of thinking and beliefs become our own cultural lens through which we view events, and may lead us to think that some cultures are irrational or inferior to our own (Ormrod, 2010).

As we attempt to encourage and serve reluctant parents, several factors should be recognized. Clearly language barriers are critical, and the need for interpreters and the understanding of culture through the lens of the parent is paramount. Transportation may also need to addressed, as many new immigrants must rely on public transportation for travel to the school sites. At times, exhausting work schedules and child-care issues for younger siblings can also be factors that decrease parent participation and contact with schools and teachers. Many parents may think it is inappropriate to ask teachers about their child's progress, and often, prior bad experiences with the school or teachers (Salend and Taylor, 1993) may inhibit the parents' confidence in contacting the school.

In each case, teachers who are truly servant leaders need to be aware of these cultural and language gaps and sensitive to the needs of these families while also being supportive of their students. Teachers can do nothing to change the conditions or cultures in which their students live, but they can work to change their own biases, as well as the institutional structures that act as obstacles to student learning (Nieto, 2003).

Variability in language and culture means teacher servants need to advocate for the disbursement of school information in multiple formats and languages. Flexibility in times and contexts for parents to meet with teachers is critical, and the understanding of multiple cultures and their families' needs and concerns, as well as advocating for students from these families when their parents and families are less connected due to language and different cultural beliefs, are all essential servant-teacher qualities. Respecting these language and culture differences is the first step in serving the families and parents of these students.

Serving the Economically Poor

Urban schools, not unlike their counterparts in other types of communities across our country that include poor rural populations, can and must be places where children and adults thrive and are cared for, and where every single child has the potential to achieve success (Donnell, 2010). Public school teachers and schools are in place to serve every student and family that walks through the door, regardless of race, gender, religious affiliation, and income level. This attitude of serving others represents the concept of "unconditional positive regard" in that servant teachers accept all students unconditionally, disregarding their tattered clothes, matted hair, poor hygiene, and, at times, language, odor, and perhaps what appears to be apathy and disrespect, with the ever-present goal to understand and serve their needs. Although understanding the issues surrounding poverty and the needs of students and families from this population are critical and could reasonably fill several books, for now our focus is on briefly discussing these issues and what teachers can do to serve this population.

Payne (2001) and others (Jensen, 2009) have suggested two important factors that differentiate poverty issues: the difference in situational poverty and generational poverty. Situational poverty is defined to be shorter in length and is caused by specific circumstances that create an immediate lack of financial resources. Situational poverty could result from the illness or death of a primary caregiver, the sudden loss of job to economic crises, or perhaps a divorce. With situational poverty, families and individuals may have an attitude of pride and a refusal to accept any type of charity or assistance.

Individuals suffering from situational poverty often bring more resources to their specific situation in that there may be supportive family members or support groups that can assist if the situation comes to a crisis point. Victims of situational poverty also know the "rules" of at least the middle- or higher-income class since at one time they lived with a higher level of income.

In contrast, generational poverty is defined as having been in poverty for at least two or more generations. Those that suffer from generational poverty tend to have fewer resources and support groups and also tend to rely on public or governmental assistance.

Some researchers would also suggest that those suffering from generational poverty have an attitude of continuing despair to the point of lacking the ability to see or envision a potentially better outcome, and an attitude that "the world owes them a living" (Payne, 2001). Payne also suggests that those in generational poverty don't understand or know the "formal rules" of the next-higher social class, and therefore have little chance of moving toward a better financial circumstance.

Although some would argue with Payne's interpretation and analysis (Bomer, Dworin, May, and Semingson, 2008; Gorski, 2006; Ng and Rury, 2006; Osei-Kofi, 2005), suggesting that she supports a classic example of deficit thinking (discussed later in this chapter), most would agree that children from poverty are often identified and labeled with grossly overgeneralized, deficit-laden characteristics that put them at risk of being less capable, less cultured, and less worthy learners (Sato and Lensmire, 2009). Sato and Lensmire also suggest that if we expect teachers to serve students from diverse backgrounds that include poverty-stricken families, we first must challenge current misinformation and focus on children's competency, the teacher's cultural identity, and professional development that encourages a true and valid understanding of poverty and its impact on students, learning styles, and the collaborative effort among teachers to support these families and students.

Because of their environments, poor children are often not read to aloud as young children and are not exposed to complex language and large vocabularies. Their parents often have lower-wage jobs, often suffer frequent job relocation that can result in family stress, apply arbitrary discipline in the home, and live in neighborhoods that have more crime and drug problems and fewer role models with professional careers. Their opportunities for vacations or trips to educational sites (museums, zoos, etc.) and participation in extracurricular activities are often limited. Each of these factors or disadvantages begins to have a cumulative effect, but they do not indicate that poor students are not intelligent or that poor students can't achieve at high levels.

We do know the following key statistics about those who suffer from poverty circumstances and the challenges that they ultimately face. In the United States in 1996, one in four individuals under the age of eighteen was living in poverty. In 1989, one in three Latino children was living in poverty (Miranda, 1991). Regardless of race or ethnicity, poor children are much more likely than non-poor children to suffer developmental delay, to drop out of high school, and to give birth during the teen years (Miranda, 1991).

Poor children are more likely to be in single-parent homes and seven times more likely to be the victims of child abuse or neglect (Renchler, 1993).

Children under the age of six remain especially vulnerable to poverty, as those living in families with a female householder and no husband present experienced poverty rates of 50.3 percent, more than five times the rate of children in married-couple families (U.S. Bureau of the Census, 1999; Payne, 2001). Poverty rates for Native American children (39.8 percent), Hispanic children (30.3 percent), and African American children (33.1 percent) are much greater than poverty rates for white children (13.5 percent) (U.S. Bureau of the Census, 1999).

These types of statistical numbers are overpowering in the sense that poverty among children is at an alarming rate. This makes the issue for teachers even more important in terms of how they can effectively serve a population that has so many obstacles in their path.

Deficit and Alternative Paradigms

Information from standardized test results, federal educational reform movements, media headlines, and pontificating politicians may have convinced teachers that urban, poor, ethnically diverse schools are in a state of crisis in the United States. This may be true in some cases, and these legitimate concerns are at the forefront of school board meetings and political platforms. Unfortunately, the intense attention to this perceived crisis belies that fact that many urban schools are thriving (Donnell, 2010). Many, without exception, are effective, caring, just, and truly strive for success for all the children in their buildings and districts.

It is true that urban, poor, public schools have struggled historically due to a lack of funding, inappropriate staffing, and inefficient and dehumanizing bureaucracies (Donnell, 2010). Additional factors that often contribute to their apparent struggles can be attributed to differences in the demographic profiles of teacher and student populations; the increasing populations of non-English-speaking or limited-English-speaking students; continuing gaps in academic achievement and completion rates among racial, cultural, and economically poor students; and severe problems in the recruitment and retention of teachers in these poor urban settings.

Often, these struggling schools recruit the newest teachers with the least experience, and when opportunities arise for transfers to less challenging schools, these teachers move on and the cycle continues, with newer recruits again honing their skills at sites where the best and most experienced teachers are sorely needed.

Being a successful teacher and one that has a servant-leader mentality requires an understanding of all of these conditions and factors that impact urban schools and challenging student populations. At times, this sense of crisis and the understanding of these factors reinforce what some have claimed to be a deficit paradigm (Donnell, 2010; Bomer, Dworin, May, and Semingson, 2008; Sato and Lensmire, 2009; Harry and Klinger, 2007). A deficit paradigm is one where children, their families, and sometimes their communities are seen as deficient and blamed for their lack of success. As teachers, if we believe and encourage a deficit paradigm orientation, we believe that student academic failure is due to specific, alleged, internal deficiencies like a lack of intelligence or specific dysfunctional family situations.

Although specific family situations may contribute to the challenge of educating urban children, suggesting that urban children and their families are always responsible for their failure is counterproductive and fails to accentuate the positive and powerful opportunities that exist in urban education. As Donnell (2010) has suggested, when we acknowledge that there is nothing "wrong" or "deficit" with urban students and their families or communities, we might begin to ask if the problem has been in the type of schools we have been providing for them for a multitude of years.

In an attempt to serve parents and families, particularly those in urban districts, educators need to be convinced of the possibility of an alternative paradigm that is in contrast to the deficit model. One example is an ecological paradigm that conceptualizes school life and classroom teaching as occurring within interconnected webs of settings and institutions that go beyond classrooms and school borders. Schools, children, and their families that live in specific communities and neighborhoods are embedded in the community, and therefore are influenced by socioculturally organized environments. More so than single factors like student misbehavior or outdated textbooks, the interconnected ecological system that includes the school, family, community, and society has a greater impact on schooling and more potential to work in tandem to serve students than any one specific factor.

With regard to urban, diverse schools, an ecological paradigm or model recognizes the interconnectedness of children, language, urban policy, poverty, customs, religion, classrooms, and culture and how these entities influence each other in bidirectional complexities. In the case of urban schools, they are embedded in a much larger context, one that requires multiple sectors of the community to work together in support of schools, teachers, and children. The teacher, students, and their families, the school, or even the school district alone cannot bring about meaningful change. Together, however, they can create highly successful schools that ensure achievement for all students and that, in the long run, function as a service to their communities (Donnell, 2010).

Effectively serving parents and families from an ecological paradigm suggests that teachers must not only support the needs of these stakeholders, but they must also consider the potential utilization of the wealth of diversity and of the cultural and personal resources that students and their families potentially bring to urban schools. They must also learn to value diverse cultural and religious backgrounds, as well as first languages and those that are spoken in the home. These teachers must also recognize that students bring cultural and cognitive resources to the classroom and that these resources can be used to provide meaningful learning experiences that tap into prior knowledge and experiences.

The belief that every child can succeed at high academic levels cannot be rooted in the current rhetoric of high standards and more standardized testing, but in the belief that all children are naturally inclined to explore, imagine, discover, and interact at a high level of engagement. Teachers must serve parents and families by encouraging them to have a strong shared vision for their child and by helping them understand that there are ways and opportunities to engage in schools so that everyone achieves.

Servant teachers serve parents and families best by helping them to understand this interconnected web and by gaining a commitment to consider and determine not *if* their child can be academically successful, but with their help, *how* they can be successful. Care and respect for children and their families begins with a desire to serve and should be viewed as ethical accountability, not sentimentality. Building caring school communities that are willing to serve students and their families is not easy, and must be viewed as a process of co-participation and activity with other people and with community resources. However, the teacher that is committed to service understands that learning is situated in particular contexts and settings and resists the separation of school and the everyday world of students. The worlds of school, family, and community are one and inseparable when it comes to learning and effectively serving families and their children in that community.

The majority of parents want what is best for their children and recognize the value of a good education. Therefore, it is essential that they are not left out of the loop when we are concerned about their children and their performance in school. As we converse and continue to serve children and their parents, we must listen to their attitudes and opinions with an open mind and try to find common ground on which to develop strategies for helping their children thrive in the classroom.

CHAPTER SIX

~

The Teacher as Servant Leader to Colleagues and the School Administration

Leaders we admire do not place themselves at the center; they place others there. They do not seek the attention of people; they give it to others. They do not focus on satisfying their own aims and desires; they look for ways to respond to the needs and interests of their constituents. They are not self-centered; they concentrate on the constituent . . . Leaders serve a purpose and the people who have made it possible for them to lead. . . . In serving a purpose, leaders strengthen credibility by demonstrating that they are not in it for themselves; instead, they have the interests of the institution, department, or team and its constituents at heart. Being a servant may not be what many leaders had in mind when they chose to take responsibility for the vision and direction of their organization or team, but serving others is the most glorious and rewarding of all leadership tasks.

—Kouzes and Posner

Never in the history of American education has the job of the school principal and the teachers that serve the larger educational community been so closely reviewed and scrutinized by their citizens, shareholders, and public officials. With greater accountability, this scrutiny continues to take the form of standardized testing results as the central measure of effective teachers, administrators, and schools. This chapter is not a critical critique of federal policy in regard to testing and assessment, although there is plenty of room for this type of analysis that would take up volumes of space. Instead, this

*Natural divide: Labor — Mgnt
Faculty - Staff - Admin*

chapter focuses on the teacher as a servant leader to their colleagues, principals, and administrators of the school.

There has typically been a long-standing distrust between administrators and teachers, illustrated by the fact that principals often only observe and have extended contact with teachers and their classrooms when it is time to evaluate them. This, in turn, can create an atmosphere where teachers take a suspicious view of administrators and of being observed and evaluated (Stigler and Hiebert, 1999). This mistrust often ruins one of teachers' richest learning opportunities—the opportunity to observe the practice of others and to gain feedback concerning their own pedagogy, practice, and growth. Given this lack of true or perceived trust, the role of the teacher in the form of servant to their colleagues and administration becomes important to define.

Promoting a Culture of Collegiality

Teachers are always encouraged to promote the development of collegiality and openness to new ideas and creative collaboration. We typically think of the principal as the encourager of these characteristics among their faculty since we know that reflecting on teacher practices, sharing instructional ideas with colleagues, and experimenting with new ideas in the classroom are all positive indicators of a learning community that is growing and ever-improving its ability to serve students (Hord and Sommers, 2008; Killion and Roy, 2009; Leithwood, 1990; Raywid, 1993). However, the servant teacher can also encourage these characteristics of collegiality by helping to promote and develop a sense of mutual respect within the school environment.

Everyone wants to be treated with respect and to be considered a valued, contributing member to the school community. The most effective teachers don't see poor student achievement and difficult student behavior as inadequacies or deficits within their students, but rather opportunities to address problems and to consider proactive methods to better serve students. Teachers who consider their fellow teachers and the administration or school principal as true colleagues can also work in a proactive sense to solve school environment problems and to create a collegial learning atmosphere. The way individuals perceive themselves being treated by others can lead to increased or decreased conflict, and thus can support or inhibit a sense of collegiality.

Many scholars would debate the issue of whether an organization's culture can be deliberately influenced by the actions of its leaders (Seyfarth,

1999). If organizational and school culture is constantly evolving and influenced by a number of factors both internal and external to the organization, it begins to suggest that the school principal may be only one of several factors that influence the school community and the opportunity for a collegial environment. In this sense, the leadership of the school or the principal may play a major role in potentially impacting the school and learning environment.

Others (Angus, 1996) have suggested that the environmental culture of the school is a characteristic of the group collective, and not a manipulatable variable. With this argument, the principal can have little impact on the school environment that the teachers and students have already created as a collective group or learning community. As a collective force, however, teachers within a building can also impact the learning environment, and along with the administration, can develop a sense of collegiality that not only provides a place for students to learn academics, but also provides them an opportunity to see examples of collaborative effort.

As a teacher servant leader, the goal of democratic teaching in terms of developing collaboration and collegiality among students, fellow teachers, and the administration should focus on breaking down barriers, overcoming obstacles, and opening doors, minds, and possibilities, with the ultimate outcome of empowering and enabling every stakeholder (Ayers, 2004). As teachers that support collegiality and strive to assist the administration to also support collegiality, respect for colleagues and valuing opinions and perspectives of others is the first step to developing the ability to see and alter the school environment. It also allows us to begin to understand, and also to reinvent, our school climates to those of collaborative and collegial environments that promote a sense of community ownership and educational responsibility.

Facilitating Creativity and Teamwork

"Creating a school climate in which creativity and teamwork are encouraged and in which teachers and administrators work and grow together is a challenging task and a job for which most teachers and school leaders are not trained" (Hoerr, 2005, 106). Everyone in the school environment must share an attitude of respect, treating each other with care and consideration. Although the traditional top-down hierarchical nature of leadership remains a reality of different titles and roles, with each player having different responsibilities, these differences should not have a major impact on how individuals should interact with one another. A custodian, teacher's

Tethered Balloon image →
* Tendencies of Organizations — Good great good.—
Can be bad!

70 ~ Chapter Six

aide, bus driver, school nurse, school counselor, case worker, teacher, administrator, and student each plays a vital role in the school structure, and fairness of treatment and mutual respect are the first steps in developing an environment of teamwork, collaboration, and creativity within the school.

A traditional authoritarian leadership style creates a hierarchy that never makes anyone feel good, except the people at the very top (Wetlaufer, 2000, 60). The hierarchical structure of businesses and, unfortunately, schools often creates distance among people in organizations when thoughtless decisions are made without input from others and when leaders fail to understand the relationship between themselves and their subordinates. Developing teamwork and creative opportunities requires respect and trust that are often developed over time and where consistent beliefs and actions from all parties nurture an environment of respect and confidence.

From the teacher's perspective, part of encouraging teamwork is being supportive of your colleagues and the administrator and developing a confidence in their leadership and decision-making skills. Hopefully this confidence is reciprocated from them and the administrator if they truly desire a school environment that is team-focused, where decisions that are made are best for the school and its students. In developing a team atmosphere, teachers should feel comfortable bringing concerns and questions to their fellow teachers and the administration, without fear of rumors and negative innuendo in the workroom or hallway. Teachers also have to follow through with commitments and take responsibility when bad decisions or errors have been made. Likewise, the administration has to share equal responsibility. Consistent actions from both teachers and administrators help both parties to predict potential reactions to both conflict and positive outcomes and help to develop a collaborative environment of teamwork.

Fostering creativity and teamwork does not happen overnight. From undergraduate teacher education programs to advanced degree programs, teachers and administrators often have little to no training in team building and outside-the-box thinking. Wagner (2001) has even suggested that with few opportunities to work with adults during the workday, many educators have not developed the skills of teamwork. Even with a good, congenial faculty, we have no guarantee that a faculty of teachers and support staff will work together toward the common good. Although we know that effective leadership has to be encouraged from the principal and requires team building among teachers, competing demands for the principal's time include concerned parents, administrative reports, teacher concerns, and addressing

* You go first — TRUST, RISK, Reach out —
* Create a deep current

student behavior. The true teacher servant can support the administration and their colleagues by encouraging collaborative teamwork, creative thinking, and problem solving among each of these stakeholders.

Listening to one another is the first step to respecting one another's opinions. Servant teachers should work hard to discuss and engage their colleagues in conversations about collegiality. They should explore productive ways to provide each other and the administration productive feedback. They should also value and nurture relationships through trust, empowerment, and high expectations.

In terms of the teacher-administrator relationship and their communication, everyone must be given the time and opportunity to be heard (Hoerr, 2005). Even the best principals in the most collaborative and creative schools can fall into the trap of being isolated and far removed from teacher and student concerns. The teacher servant who is supportive of the administration has to have the courage to share information with the principal and to tell them what they need to know. This can be done without being seen as a malcontent or complainer, but more as a concerned, supportive faculty member who wants to be candid and honest about the environment of the school.

The principal is, in fact, in charge of the building and also evaluates teachers on an annual basis, but the principal who can encourage the development of true learning communities and who can encourage honest feedback without the threat of retribution is one who sets the stage for a collaborative team effort and opens the doors for creative thinking and problem solving. The teacher's role is to be a supportive team member without the fear of making mistakes. But teachers also have to send this same message to their administrator that mistakes are part of the learning and growth process.

As part of a collaborative team, creative teachers and administrators will try new strategies and be comfortable with mistakes that are bound to occur. They are supportive of each other and will continue to experiment and brainstorm to seek better ways to serve students. Sharing successes and mistakes with one another (both teachers and principals) helps to develop an open atmosphere where other colleagues can learn from their mistakes and where students also eventually see that creativity, reflection, and making mistakes are part of the deeper understanding of the learning process. Keeping good teachers and administrators who can make a difference in students' lives helps to create a setting where everyone has the potential to grow and learn. This can only happen when trust, respect, teamwork, and collaboration are the norm (Hoerr, 2005).

Building Learning Communities

Building learning communities is currently a popular phrase in the research literature that explores schools and the promotion of effective learning environments. To say that an organization or a school is a learning community is to suggest that each stakeholder has an emotional and professional tie to one another and that they are somewhat linked by shared values, beliefs, and mutual dependence (Raywid, 1993). Collaborative professional learning is a type of professional development in which both teachers and administrators work together to improve teaching, learning, and the school environment (Hord and Sommers, 2008; Killion and Roy, 2009). A school and staff that embrace the learning community concept in the frame of servant leadership come together to learn within a supportive, creative, and self-created community. As such, teacher and administrator learning and support occurs in a more complex, deeper, and more fruitful social setting, where the participants can interact, test ideas that challenge their inferences and interpretations, and process new information with each other (Morrissey, 2000).

Schools with these characteristics and traits are environments where students, support staff, teachers, and administrators can express themselves and find understanding and support. Although many times school structures are not created with the specific intent to encourage or cultivate a sense of community, community building needs to be a constant focus if we want to create positive relationships while supporting academic and achievement motivation and feelings of self-esteem and self-worth within the school community. If educators are to enhance their organizational capacity, boost student learning, and improve their ability to serve, they should work on building professional learning communities that are characterized by shared purpose; collaborative activity with students, colleagues, and the administration; and collective responsibility among staff members (Newmann and Wehlage, 1995).

True and effective learning communities are simply characterized by professional collaboration, disciplined intent to make a difference and to search for solutions in the school environment, and ongoing assessment. "Teachers do not learn best from outside experts or by attending conferences or implementing programs installed by outsiders. Teachers learn best from other teachers in settings where they literally teach each other the art of teaching. For this to happen, collaboration has to work in a radically different way" (Little, 2005, 141–142). This productive collaboration must be focused, rather than casual or general, and must be supported by frequent and continuous communication about teaching and practice. In terms of service, it must also involve an understanding of how each member in the learning community can support and serve the greater school environment and, ultimately, the learning and development of children.

McMillan and Chavis (1986) proposed four characteristics of schools that contribute to enhancing feelings of community: (1) membership, (2) reinforcement, (3) influence, and (4) shared emotional connection. The central question, then, is how do teachers serve their colleagues and the administration by promoting a sense of community within these four constructs?

Membership can be defined as the shared sense of belonging and personal relatedness to a specific group. Membership supports ownership and helps members to feel connected to others, begins the process to develop identity, and sets the groundwork to develop emotional security. Membership is also the key to persuading reluctant students to try to succeed in school (Newmann, Wehlage, and Lamborn, 1992). Principals are well-served if they can influence this sense of membership within their school environment in both teachers and students; however, teachers can also encourage this atmosphere of membership. Helping a new colleague or principal to feel at home and assisting them to acquire a sense of belonging in their new school community is just as important as helping new students to the classroom to become accepted and adjusted.

Helping to reduce the sense of social distance between the teacher and administrator that we know tends to exist and personalizing the experience through interacting frequently with colleagues and administrators in a variety of ways other than prescribed by official roles is one of the first steps in serving school colleagues by developing a sense of community. By de-emphasizing the nature of unhealthy competition and by quickly integrating the "new" faculty or principal into the school community membership, the process of bonding and sense of one vision can begin to develop.

Reinforcement occurs in the form of integration and need fulfillment in a behaviorist sense. Schools where students, faculty, and administrators are friendly and supportive of one another have high cohesiveness, which refers to the extent to which all of these stakeholders express positive feelings about their peers and provide both psychological and emotional support of one another (Fraser, Anderson, and Walberg, 1982). When teachers and administrators can encourage cohesiveness and work together to establish curriculum or behavioral expectations of the school community, both parties begin to reinforce one another by sharing cooperatively common goals. This, in effect, provides feedback and reinforcement and begins to provide a common-ground landscape where both teachers and administrators can be honest and express positive feelings about the growth of the school and the

acceptance of everyone's position and role in building, supporting, and serving the school community.

From the teacher's perspective as a servant leader, encouraging a sense of
community membership through reinforcement and support of colleagues
and the administration does not represent automatic agreement or compliance, and it does not silence the teacher's ability to express disagreement
with policy or goals. But by helping to establish this sense of community,
acceptance, and respect of everyone's unique position, it does begin to set
the stage for an environment where conflicts and disagreements can become
discussions and brainstorming activities to discover solutions to problems in
the school community.

Belonging to a school community includes the possibility and very likely
probability of having a specific influence on students, colleagues, and the
school administrator. By influencing the school community either directly
or indirectly, teachers have the unique opportunity to impact the school
environment and the relationships that exist. As Hank Levin has stated,
"Our view . . . is that if you can't make a school a great professional place for
staff, it's never going to be a great place for kids" (in Brant, 1992, 21). In a
true community sense, influence should be reciprocal, where every member's
opinion is respected and where individuals feel that they matter to the group.
Teachers need to remember and understand that their colleagues and administrators are an integral part of the school climate, culture, and community,
and the better they are at serving and developing positive relationships with
each other, the closer the school will come to being a psychologically healthy
place to work and develop. This is not always an easy task, as some administrators (as well as teachers) are more difficult to work with than others.

As teachers, we also have "easy" and more difficult students to work with
each year, but our goal is to regard them as positive citizens of our class with
an unconditional acceptance. Likewise, servant teachers need to accept the
leadership of the administrator and their colleagues unconditionally while
trying to encourage a greater school environment of healthy collaboration
and support. Having a positive influence of support that is genuine and respectful helps to promote cohesiveness and begins to validate one's identity
as a group member (McMillan & Chavis, 1986). The positive influence and
the servant attitude we can have as teachers go beyond the classroom and
our students and reach to other school staff members and administrators,
ultimately helping to encourage a shared community vision and healthy
educational climate.

A shared emotional connection is the definitive element of a true community (Seyfarth, 1999). This emotional connection may be based on a

shared history of earlier events, accomplishments, or losses, or in the school setting, a shared strong value of tradition and shared values and goals. By encouraging and developing a sense of community membership, reinforcing and providing positive feedback for growth, and influencing one another, a shared emotional connection can begin to form among all stakeholders of the school environment.

As teachers, we encourage students to develop a sense of social responsibility for their peers and the classroom as a true learning community where we share an emotional connection to help all students to improve their self-regulation, self-confidence, and self-worth. We are emotionally tied to students in terms of their academic achievement and in terms of their psychological, physical, and mental health. It therefore comes as no surprise that teachers as servant leaders can actually impact this same emotional connection to their school administration and colleagues.

Refusing to participate in negative teacher-workroom tactics and conversations targeted against the administration or others is a positive start toward developing a sense of community and encouraging a climate of shared vision and emotional support of one another. Refusing to make negative or derogatory comments about the administration or other teachers in the presence of children is another strategy to engender feelings of a learning community's self-worth and pride of accomplishment. It only takes a few voices to begin the rumors of negativity and discord.

We frequently remind students to behave in ways that give positive credit to the school and that they are representatives of the school community, so during assemblies and field trips, we encourage them to be on their best behavior so that the school is not reflected upon negatively. As servant teachers, we should also think of ourselves as representatives of our school and profession. Making negative comments or being non-supportive of school employees, students, students' families, and the administration, either within the school or in the community, only helps to destroy the sense of collegiality and, eventually, the shared emotional connection to the school and its stakeholders.

Civility

All schools operate more smoothly when administrators, teachers, paraprofessionals, and students behave and act with predictable behavior and patterns. The expectations of a smooth efficient and predictable school environment emerge as a byproduct of this interdependence among members of work groups and the civil collaboration of everyone involved. In schools where teachers have little interaction with colleagues or administrators and where each carries out duties in isolation, interdependence is low and work-related expectations are sparse. When teachers and administrators collaborate as members of a supportive team, interdependence and mutual cooperation are more common (Peterson and Brietzke, 1994).

This being said, school environments and the behavior of students, teachers, and administrators are seldom predictable and can often follow uncommon and unpredictable patterns of disobedience, disrespect, and distrust. Maintaining a congenial demeanor and cooperative attitude while also encouraging co-workers and students to achieve excellence are part of the delicate dance of the norm and expectation of civility. To some extent, this expectation of civility is highly valued in most organizations (Lee, Bryk, and Smith, 1993) and in the school environment. The norm of civility in schools and the expectations that teachers have to serve the public and the administration dictate that teachers attend to others' feelings and avoid acts or words that might be offensive or hurtful to others (Seyfarth, 1999; White, 1996).

Along with these goals and expectations, civility also calls for the routine expression of interest in others' welfare (Lee, Bryk, and Smith, 1993) and includes an attitude of tolerance of other people's behavior and beliefs, even when they may differ from their own expectations (Hoover and Kindsvatter, 1997). In the school environment, we often can observe islands of civility surrounded by a sea of indifference, which leads both administrators and teachers to identify ways and opportunities to break down walls and remove barriers (Seyfarth, 1999). It should be the desire of servant teachers to support one another and to work toward the goal of creating a civil educational environment in both the classroom and the school.

Students normally have clear ideas about the behavior they like and dislike in their teachers, and teachers and administrators also normally have clear expectations for each other in terms of expected behaviors, attitudes, and respect. It is no surprise that with each of these stakeholders, their expectations often rate favorably with those traits and characteristics associated with civility. Many of the same traits that students desire of their teachers, administrators also desire of their teachers. Students desire friendly, kind, and helpful behavior and appreciate teachers with a sense of humor who can also make classes and information understandable and interesting (Seyfarth, 1999). They also dislike petty rules and rigid restrictions that allow teachers to uncommonly or unrealistically maintain control, power, or order in the classroom (Wallace, 1996).

Students also attach a particular importance to fairness in the way they are treated and in the way that teachers enforce and interpret rules (Batcher, 1981). By the same token, teachers like to be treated kindly and fairly by their colleagues and by their supervising building administrator, with civil communication of clear rules and expectations. Colleagues and administrators who can treat teachers with honesty, respect, and civility begin to create a school environment that becomes a welcome work space. Ideally, this effort by service-oriented educators results in a trickle-down effect where teachers and administrators, in turn, treat their colleagues and students with equally civil behavior and respect.

In terms of annual performance evaluations for teachers, this event begins, at times, to place teachers and administrators at odds with one another. Not everyone can always agree on definitions of fairness, work ethic, and excellence in the classroom, and teacher and administrative expectations can begin to diverge. Since teachers are on the front lines, they are expected to serve students and to make decisions to support the welfare of their class, while at the same time supporting beliefs and expectations (that they may disagree with) of the building administration and those from the central office. So, how is the teacher expected to serve students, colleagues, and the administration in a civil manner while helping to build the best learning environment that can possibly be created?

It is important to understand that treating and responding to colleagues in a civil manner does not mean that we can't express our opinion or that we give up the right to disagree. The art of disagreement using kind words and sincere concern and respect for those whom we disagree with is one of the first steps of civil discourse. Often, administrators are following procedures, demands, and curriculum or policy mandates that generate from the central office, school board, and state or federal officials. The administrator may have done their best to disagree with or argue against a particular mandate with higher authorities, to no avail, and thus is initiating or stating a demand or curriculum policy that they themselves find questionable. As teacher servants to the administration, recognizing the difficult position of the administrator and having the ability to assist them and your colleagues in civil dialogue when controversial topics arise are key.

We know that students respond better when they understand and recognize that a teacher's interest and concern for them is genuine. By the same token, administrators will respond more favorably when they understand that teachers' concerns for them are genuine and that teachers are making their best attempt to be a part of collaborative team effort, hopefully making decisions that are in the best interest of children. As teachers, our goal is to treat students fairly and with respect, but also to treat our immediate supervisor, the administrator, with the same reciprocal respect that we hope to be treated with.

The teacher-principal relationship is not destined to be one of distrust and animosity, but one of respect, openness, fairness, genuine concern, and high expectations for everyone involved. Civil respect and a willingness to serve the administration may mean volunteering to lead curriculum group discussions with colleagues, building project initiatives, or holding collaborative grade-level team meetings. It may also mean sharing concerns of the faculty in a manner that is honest and respectful, or simply making phone calls to parents to remind them of parent-teacher conferences or back-to-school nights.

In either a direct or indirect form, service to colleagues and the administration does not mean being subversive or attempting to undermine co-workers or administrative dictates. A willingness to serve, even when small disagreements exist, requires a humble attitude, a demeanor of service, and perhaps an even smaller ego, but remains part of the essential elements of creating a positive working and learning environment where we serve and support those in authority (administrators) and those that we share authority with (colleagues), with the ultimate objective of creating an environment where everyone can feel empowered to contribute and to do their best work.

CHAPTER SEVEN

~

The Teacher as Servant Leader to the Community

Community begins with a shared vision. It's sustained by teachers who, as school leaders, bring inspiration and direction to the institution. Who, after all, knows more about the classroom? Who is better able to inspire children? . . . And who but teachers can create a true community for learning? Teachers are, without question, the heartbeat of a successful school.

—Ernest Boyer (1995, 31)

Public schools are an integral part of every community in the United States. Servant teachers need to recognize that if they and the school are to serve the community effectively, they must be conscious of the local social and economic developments and, in a broader sense, the geographical area and the constituents that they serve. Pawlas (1995, 26) identified six factors that differentiate communities from one another: tradition and background, values the community holds, economic bases, geographic features, social structures, and political structures. Although some communities may have several of these traits in common, it would be rare to find two communities that have all six factors as identical. This is why to be an effective servant to the community, teachers must understand these constantly emerging issues and characteristics.

Schools do not exist apart from the community they are attempting to serve. For many small towns and communities, schools are the lifeblood and social gathering place for important events. In rural communities and even in large cities and urban environments, schools are often the one common denominator for local neighborhoods that have a common stake and interest in the development of a healthy community and its children. One of the key factors of public relations—or for our discussion, service to the community—is the concept of social accountability (Yeager, 1985).

Just as a business that begins to provide a service to the community has a social responsibility to understand the needs of the community, schools have a similar responsibility to be socially accountable. Public relations and community service denote more than simple customer service; in actuality, these mean accountability to one's public. Therefore, social accountability from the perspective of public education represents our accountability to all the publics we serve, which include but are not limited to teachers, students, parents, the neighborhood, non-parents, senior citizens, churches, businesses, and industries in the proximal area of our community. As educators, we want to create favorable and honest impressions of our schools and to garner community support for our programs and students. Establishing positive school and community relationships can be accomplished with the attitude and effort of educators to see themselves as servant leaders of the local community.

Tradition and Cultural Background

To serve a community effectively, schools and teachers must understand the specific traditions and cultural backgrounds of their specific neighborhood communities. In effect, constituents of a community may have a wide variety of interests, different kinds of jobs, varied political views, different religious beliefs, diverse racial and nationality backgrounds, and very different views of what schools and teachers should be doing and what their roles should be in the educational process. Understanding that communities are quickly becoming more diverse in terms of tradition and culture, and understanding our own assumptions about different groups of people in our communities becomes increasingly more important.

The community may shift rapidly as neighborhoods change, as new school attendance zones are created, as jobs are lost, as urban renewal creates a different kind of clientele or no immediate clientele, as schools and businesses open and close and populations are combined, as ethnic racial composition changes drastically, and as English is discovered not to be the primary language spoken in the majority of homes (Hughes and Ubben, 1994, 66). Understanding these subtle or rapid changes within the community not only helps teachers to understand their students' experiences outside of the classroom, but it also helps to put their students' world in context for the teacher.

Understanding the differences in a school community surrounded by an agrarian and agricultural economy where the population is homogenous and where the year is centered on the weather, planting and harvesting crops, as opposed to a poor urban school community where ethnic diversity and community center around public transportation, public housing, city parks, ghettos, and thriving or failing businesses that result in poor job prospects, provides different contexts for the teacher to understand. Servant teachers not only understand the children they teach, but also understand the dynamic interaction between them and their community and the influences within that impact students, both positively and negatively.

If a community for many years has been comprised of a majority, white, Christian, middle- to upper-class group of residents and these demographics suddenly change due to economic stress, loss of jobs, and perhaps the relocation of jobs and therefore families, teachers need to be aware of these changes so that they can more clearly serve the community population that currently surrounds the school. Poorer families may not have as much access to the school or feel confident in approaching school personnel, especially if the lack of English skills is a limitation for communication. Understanding potential new traditions, cultural expectations, and the needs of students and their parents in effect serves the needs of the community. As new businesses open and community opportunities arise, it is critical for teachers and administrators to communicate with these groups and organizations and to determine what their partnerships and coordinated efforts can provide them in terms of service to encourage a community effort of excellence in supporting children and their needs.

Progress in education today relies in large part on the cooperation of parents, businesses, and other community patrons, as well as understanding the role of community agencies and government entities. Teachers, who have their fingers on the pulse of the community and understand the expectations of the constantly changing demographics of their students and patrons, have an opportunity to serve the community by doing everything they can to support students' academic, social, and psychological needs.

Community Values

Progress in education today depends a great deal on consensus building with input from parents and other citizens of the community. This consensus building also includes the maintenance of understanding community agencies at the local, state, and national levels within the government structure. But more importantly, as servants, it requires that educators understand the values within the community. The values that are most important are not necessarily those of a formal nature in terms of power and influence, but those of an informal nature that impact the daily lives of families and community members.

As more and more communities experience hard times economically, and as these communities experience large demographic changes in terms of families who are immigrants or foreign born, educators must understand the values of these ever-changing communities. The world we live in today is extremely diverse; therefore, the values within our communities are becoming more differentiated on a yearly basis. The current world population is 56 percent Asian, 21 percent European, 9 percent African, 8 percent South American, and 6 percent North American. The religious affiliations of the world are equally diverse, with 30 percent affiliated with Christianity, 19.5 percent Muslim, 13.8 percent Hindu, 8.5 percent Buddhist, 5.7 percent Animist, and 22.5 percent with no affiliation or with beliefs in atheism (Comillion, 1991; Hodgekinson, 1988; Jackson, 1988; Johnson and Packard, 1987).

Although the United States has often been seen as a leader in diversity issues due to its historical heritage and diverse groups of citizens (Baptiste and Hughes, 1993), past practices of valuing diversity and culture have not necessarily been successful (Hughes, 1999). The primary strategy of assimilation has often been the *modus operandi*, one in which sameness has been valued rather than diversity and where the beliefs, values, customs, and causes of the dominant group have superseded smaller minority groups. However, by the twenty-first century, people of color are predicted to outnumber whites in the United States for the first time, and this evolution will undoubtedly alter everything we have come to understand about diversity, assimilation, and culture. This evolution will also have a profound impact on the needs of schools and communities, and the teachers that continue to serve in this capacity.

This fast-emerging shift of diversity—and ultimately of values—within our communities continues to create pressure to conform, tension, role confusion, exclusion, isolation, and ethnic and economic class tension that at times leads to misunderstanding and often violent outcomes (Hughes, 1999). The high school graduation class of 2010 (which was the first-grade class of 1999) has experienced and continues to experience more diversity of values, customs, and cultures than any previous generation. Hodgekinson (1985) has suggested that among students graduating in the current decade, 24 percent were born into poverty, 14 percent were born handicapped or exceptional by the definitions outlined in the federal mandate of Public Law 92-142, and 40 percent were classified as culturally different, meaning learners other than Caucasian or of European descent who have English as a first language.

While the public school student profile becomes quite diverse, the teaching profession is actually transforming into an increasingly monoracial, monocultural, and monolingual population, becoming composed mainly of Caucasians with middle- to upper-middle-class backgrounds (Hughes, 1999). To be servants of their communities, educators must not only understand issues of cross-racial and cross-ethnic teaching, but they must also understand the unique customs and values of their school's community.

Understanding the values of the community represents a pluralistic attempt to serve many publics, each with its own values, history, and orientations. Serving the community means understanding ethnic and religious holidays (i.e. Chinese New Year, Ramadan, Cinco de Mayo, Kwanzaa, Hanukah) if these events are significant events in the culture of the community. Both cultural and religious events become a part of the fabric of the neighborhoods where schools exist and include important social and family activities that bring citizens together in unity and harmonious celebration. Understanding the physical needs of the community is just as important. Recognizing locations of public transportation, medical clinics, public assistance sites, food and clothing banks, religious worship centers, and other necessary entities within urban school neighborhoods is the first step in understanding the needs of the children teachers serve and the needs of their families. The values that a school's neighborhood community places on religion, money, education, food, athletics, music and the arts, jobs, and family are just a few of the multiple values that teachers should consider.

Serving the community represents an understanding of these values and calls for focusing our attention not only on our curriculum and instruction at the school but also on understanding how we can support and respect these values that are the lifeline of the community. Our school classrooms are an extension of the greater community, and by serving and understanding the critical values of the community, we become better servants to our students and their families. By embracing diversity within the community and respecting the values of the local neighborhood and its citizens, we can begin to respect and appreciate the efforts, struggles, and accomplishments of our students in a meaningful way through interpreting their growth in context of the larger community.

Economic Bases

Even as the current economic situation in the United States continues to slowly improve at this writing, communities will continue to face difficult financial times, with the outlook for jobs and economic growth at marginal levels. Difficult economies have a direct impact on schools and their immediate communities but also can have an extreme detrimental impact on children and their families. Serving neighborhoods and communities means understanding values and expectations of constituents, but also understanding the economic bases and resources that are available.

Funds from tax revenues and local property tax assessments seldom cover all of the school's operational costs, and principals and teachers, at times, must seek out other sources to sustain effective and important programs. Some of the general responsibilities of the school administrator are to understand the school budget, distribute resources that are allocated by the central office, and potentially generate additional revenue from donations and funding sources within the community. As teachers, we seldom control these needed financial resources, but as servants of the community, we can come to a greater understanding of financial bases and resources that exist in the neighborhood. Understanding the economic pulse of the school community, school families, and businesses and industries within the community is one of the first steps in serving students and their immediate community.

If the industrial plant in your community suddenly closes or experiences worker layoffs, families and students at your school site may be directly impacted economically and financially. Increases in free and reduced lunch status for students and potential conversions of your school to a federal Title I status will have a dramatic impact on everyone at the school site. As Payne (2001) has suggested, poverty and its impact on children may be greatly determined by the difference in situational poverty, which is determined by an immediate or sudden situation (such as an unexpected job loss), or in generational poverty, which is defined as poverty for two generations or more. In each case, needs of students and families are potentially different, and available resources also vary beyond the bounds of financial need.

Knowing the financial needs of the community and its students allows teachers and administrators to understand what special programs and services are needed for students and what community resources could potentially be of service. In addition, it also allows opportunities for schools and their teachers and students to provide services to those in need within the community. Whether it be a collection of food resources to be donated to the community food bank for the homeless or having children travel to a senior center to interact with the elderly, service to the community is a global school community opportunity to serve the neighborhood and its citizens.

Understanding the needs of the local community, as well as your own school community citizens, in times of crises allows students and teachers to understand the importance of service to others. In effect, as we have our students serve, we serve the community by encouraging and developing students who can go beyond a view of life that does not simply focus on their own personal interests, but on the interests of others.

As teachers, we are composers (or, at the least, encouragers) of student experiences, and we become more capable of effectively doing this when we understand the community needs from both a financial and personal perspective. The students' educational environment is more than the school classroom; it involves their home, community center, church, synagogue or temple, city parks, and anywhere that experiences and learning take place within the community. Serving and understanding the community needs from an economic perspective is vital to serving all of the entities within the community that impact and influence our students on a daily basis.

Geographic Features

In times of war and conflict, generals and their armies attempt to make an assessment of the battlefield or points of military engagement. This information is gathered not only to understand the enemy and its resources, but also to understand one's own needs and resources and to understand the geography of the battle zone, with the goal of giving combat troops the best chance for success. The engagement of a battle in a densely forested jungle in Vietnam is different than engaging in a military conflict in the deserts of Iraq or mountainous barren regions in Afghanistan. In the same sense, when politicians run for office, their campaign managers understand the geography of the region they attempt to help their candidate win and have a keen understanding of the geography of the region and the physical needs of the community. Schools are no different, in that the geography and natural resources of the community often dictate the health and development of the local school neighborhood. Serving local school communities also means understanding these geographic indicators and understanding the physical needs of the district.

In recent years, the geography of cities and rural communities has changed as the result of huge building developments, urban sprawl, and the relocation of families due to unemployment. Suburbs continue to grow and develop exponentially as inner-city and urban community populations become more diverse and economically poorer environments. The concept of a modern community is that of a constantly emerging social entity of which the school remains a key institution (Pawlas, 1995).

In terms of geography, having a firm grasp on the needs of the community and what residents consider important is key. In an agrarian rural community where the farming and crop industry is a vital source of employment, revenue, and family life, teachers and administrators need to understand the needs of the planting and harvest seasons and the specific needs of these families from an educational perspective and from a personal perspective. In some communities where Amish families operate their farms next to larger industrial farm operations or ever-expanding suburbs, their geographical needs are different from someone who grows up in inner-city Chicago, where understanding and using the public transit system is often vital to education, social services, and potential employment.

Geography—meaning the science that deals with the earth and its life or specific descriptions of land, sea, and air, and the distribution of plant and animal life including man and his industries—should be a central concern for school administrators and teachers as they continually seek ways to effectively serve the local community. Understanding and appreciating the geography and natural resources of the community—whether it be a community that is dependent on the fishing industry in Alaska, communities in Kansas and Oklahoma that are dependent on the annual wheat harvest, cities or communities that are dependent on specific natural resources like oil or coal, or cities whose economic base is centered on seasonal tourism—is key, as each factor plays a role in an educator's ability to serve the community.

Understanding how the geography of a local community factors into the decisions that are made by local community, business, and school leaders is critical. Helping students to understand their community and its needs while concurrently understanding the desires and expectations of the community helps to begin the discussions of how we as educators can better serve our communities and, ultimately, educate the next generation of leaders who are focused on serving others.

Social Structures

The concept of a modern community is that of a constantly changing and ever-emerging social entity of which the school is a key institution. In essence, the school's relationship to the community, state, nation, and society is a key concept to understand (Pawlas, 1995) if educators expect to serve their students and constituents effectively.

Servant educators need to understand that communities are constantly changing and that as communities change and grow, the greater the diversity of its citizens will become. In terms of social structures, Gorton and Schneider (1991) have suggested that educators should pay critical attention to several aspects of the complex community structure. Understanding the social aspects of the citizens of the community is the first step. The people of a community at times have a wide variety of interests, different jobs, different political and religious affiliations, different racial and ethnic backgrounds, and different languages spoken in the immediate home. At times this diversity of interest also represents different expectations of social behavior that can create misunderstanding and perhaps conflict in the expectations of families and the local community school.

Understanding the people of the community is important, but understanding where people in the community meet or congregate also may play a large role in understanding the social aspects of a community. Do local community leaders meet at the local coffee shop or at the community center down the street on regular occasions, or do they congregate at churches, synagogues, or temples on a weekly or daily basis? What are the typical methods of communication used in the community so that everyone becomes and remains informed about events and important issues? Is this communication by word of mouth, and does it occur in a different language than English? Is the information only communicated by certain members of a family or community? In today's world, is this information in an electronic format sent by e-mails, cell phones, text messages, Twitter pages, or social networking Internet sites? Understanding the people of the community, where these people meet, and how they communicate information to each other is important, but much of this information is centered on the expectations and attitudes of the community's citizens.

A broad spectrum of definitions currently exists for multicultural education and diversity (Banks, 1997; Bennett, 1995; Manning and Baruth, 1996; Nieto, 2003; O'Hair and Odell, 1993; Timm, 1996), and each has its own merit and aspects of validity. Because the public schools are the most common shared experience for most Americans, the United States traditionally has depended on schools to "Americanize" its citizens (Baptiste, 1999). As early as 1909, E. Cubberly (1909), a distinguished and well-respected educational leader of the day, supported the concept of forcing new immigrants in America to assimilate to their new American culture and to abandon their previous cultural heritage. Theodore Roosevelt also denounced the idea of "hyphenated Americans" (Krug, 1976, 8) and perceived names like Irish American, Asian American, or African American to be disloyal to the United States. In effect, the Americanization process was assimilation to Anglo-Saxon culture (Banks, 1997). But in the twenty-first century, the "Browning of America" will alter everything in society, from politics and education to industry, values, and cultures (Baptiste, 1999).

Even though the teaching profession is becoming increasingly monoracial, monocultural, and monolingual, being composed mainly of Caucasians with middle- to upper-middle-class income backgrounds (Baptiste, 1999), these same educators increasingly need to also understand that communities are becoming more diverse. Effectively serving their immediate communities requires an increased understanding of cross-racial, cross-ethnic social issues that involves overcoming language barriers, economic barriers, social stigmas of the homeless, stereotypes of the homosexual community, extreme poverty, the unemployed, single-parent homes, community drug and alcohol use, and gang- or community-related influences. Baptiste and Baptiste (1980) have suggested that a philosophy based on the principles of equality, recognition, and respect of human diversity, as well as a sense of moral commitment, serves as the blueprint for the emergence of a multicultural process that leads to cultural pluralism.

I would also suggest that to be true servant leaders of the local community in a social sense, educators must embrace the concept of cultural pluralism as originally defined by Kallen, (1956) and others (Appleton, 1983; Baptiste and Baptiste, 1980; Baptiste, 1999) in that in a model society or community, cultural pluralism is defined as groups from different value systems, races, religions, ethnicities, and other types of diversity coexisting in a harmonious relationship. Each of these groups is allowed to maintain its unique cultural lifestyle, and the local community—including business and community entities (that includes schools)—works together in our democratic society to promote the common values and goals of democracy.

Understanding the social structures and the citizenry of the local community; understanding the needs of community organizations, businesses, and industry; and understanding that the goal is not to "Americanize" everyone to a single definition of morals, attitudes, religion beliefs, and behavior—this may be the singular first step to understanding how one can serve the community holistically. Educating children to appreciate diverse beliefs and cultures in a social sense allows them to see themselves as future servants of the community, with the ultimate goal of creating environments that improve the welfare of all citizens of the community. Baptiste (1999) would also suggest that one of the major purposes of the public educational servant and leader is to understand the relationship of social service, multiculturalism, and character development. Public educational institutions should provide training in citizenship and pass on to youth the moral values and beliefs of the democratic way of life. These values that include fair play, concern for excellence, willingness to work hard, the ability to delay gratification, a sense of service, commitment, self-discipline, self-reliance, trust, honor, and loyalty—most of which are common to all cultures—are critical for educators to model and teach within the school climate and the local community.

Political Structures

Schooling often involves a political process. This means that what happens in schools is affected by legislative and administrative processes at the national, state, and local levels. Clearly, many of the decisions that are made at each of these levels center on budgets, money, and available resources. As hard as it is to admit this truism, power and politics go hand in hand, and as a result, decisions about how schools are governed and operated, what students should learn, who should be teaching, and how students should be taught are frequent and controversial topics of discussion. Often, when teachers can share power with students in an attempt to find a balance between teacher-centered and student-centered learning and decision making, they create more positive and enriching learning environments (Morrison, 2009). Understanding the complicated and often volatile political structures of the local community is also an important step in serving the educational and community environment.

Political acumen, or the ability to discern and perceive the political community both within the school and beyond into the broader neighborhoods and city, is an important trait to possess or acquire if educators expect to be effective servant leaders. In studies of effective school leadership, political acumen has been described in part as "knowing when to break the rules, when to short circuit the system," and knowing "when to beg for forgiveness instead of asking for permission" (Ubben and Hughes, 1997, 8). Others have suggested that effective school leaders must have the ability to cope with turbulence and be adept at using improvisation, adaptation, and flexible conflict approach/denial/avoidance and intense persuasion to maneuver within the school and community bureaucracy (Bridgeland and Duane, 1986; Blank, 1987; Chusmire and Koberg, 1987; Scotti, 1987; Keedy, 1991).

Effective educators within the school bureaucracy seem to be able to balance the inherent conflict among the attention given to teachers, individual school needs, and the central office and state legislative mandates (Hughes, 1999). Balancing this potential "political" conflict and helping the local community realize that the school belongs to them—staff, parents, students, and the community—results in the empowerment of those who are the central stakeholders of the success of the educational community. Successful school and community servant leaders have the ability to encourage everyone to work toward a common goal with a collective vision of what the school might become and, most importantly, a vision of each student's potential within the community in the very near future.

Understanding the immediate political climate becomes a central predictor of effectively serving the local school community and its surrounding neighborhoods and businesses. These stakeholders, which include parents and local community leaders, are interested in and concerned about the process of schooling and demand accountability from educators. The general public and local community are interested in education for five basic reasons (Morrison, 2009):

1. Most people have gone to school, and therefore feel that they have some understanding and knowledge of school matters.
2. Education in America is essentially viewed as being controlled and influenced by citizens who believe that one of the roles of the public schools is to educate future citizens for democratic living.
3. Many community citizens are parents, and thus they are concerned about what happens to their children in school and how this affects their children's future.
4. Citizens, who pay taxes, feel they deserve a voice in how schools operate and educate students.
5. The business community has a stake in the public schools, because they believe it is the responsibility of the public schools to prepare citizens for the workforce.

Politicians are interested in public schools for a variety of reasons. At times, candidates or those currently in office use schools as a way of implementing policy or arguing for changes that they believe are good for children and the general welfare of the state and nation. During election years, candidates may support platforms that advocate literacy, higher standards, new curriculums, class-size reductions, expanding achievement testing, and greater fiscal accountability. Businessmen and businesswomen also have a considerable vested interest in the public schools and how students are educated. They want future workers who are employable and who can perform well in the local labor force. Most businesses want workers who can think critically, ones who are good problem solvers, those who can work well with others, and those who can learn quickly and can make good decisions, both on the job and in their personal lives.

In terms of serving the community and understanding the political nature of the influence of key leaders in the community, it does not matter what political party you are affiliated with or if you tend to have conservative or liberal views on specific political, religious, or social issues. What does matter is that teachers who are servant leaders understand the political tendency of the local community and its leaders and understand how and why specific decisions are made. Serving the community may often mean attempting to understand why certain decisions are made, even if you don't agree with a particular political or moral philosophy that is being supported. It may also involve forms of protest or expressions of disagreement to ensure that decisions are made with the best interest of students in mind.

Although the leadership within schools and communities tends to be bureaucratic, successful servant leaders within the teaching ranks seem to be able to balance the inherent conflict between the bureaucracy or community political agendas and their own personal beliefs and decisions about what is best for schools and students. Knowing that you live and teach in a conservative or liberal community in terms of religious and moral beliefs should help you to understand why community politicians and even school board members want specific curricular and personnel decisions to occur within the school.

In election years, candidates from the federal level all the way down to the local school board will attempt to establish their political agendas and goals for the local educational community. Businesses, religious leaders, community activists, and influential citizens (including parents) will also establish their interests and concerns and provide their opinions and agendas for "fixing" the schools in the upcoming year. It is the responsibility of the teacher who is a servant leader to the community to understand these issues and to make and encourage decisions for productive change that are in the best interests of students, their parents, and the community.

Understanding the political landscape of the community is essential for teachers to effectively serve their communities. In the public sector, the community pays teachers' salaries and hires and fires teachers and school personnel to provide their students instruction, guidance, nurturance, and common goals of future democratic citizenship. To be an effective servant of the community, teachers must understand the tradition and backgrounds of community members and must also understand the community values that both the majority and minority members of the community represent. Effective teacher servants must also understand the economic bases of the community, which include geographic features and the social structures that heavily influence citizens and the businesses that employ families within the community.

Understanding these complex variables and how each of these are interwoven and influenced by political and personal agendas within the community is not an easy task, especially when community agendas differ from your own beliefs, customs, or moral values. However, effective teachers who have a desire to serve their stakeholders and constituents and who have a sincere interest in serving their students are able to juggle these discrepancies and continue to effectively work toward positive change and reform within the community school structure.

CHAPTER EIGHT

Conclusion

We convince by our presence.

—Walt Whitman

Who is the servant leader, and what teacher can effectively serve all of the stakeholders that have been discussed in this text? From students and parents to colleagues, administrators, and community, servant leaders lead by example and cast a large net of service and stewardship as they sacrifice, at times, their own desires and needs for the sake of those they serve. Servant leaders differ from other persons of goodwill and others with authentic good intentions because they act on what they believe. They are committed to serving others. There is a sustaining spirit when they venture and take risks to do the "right" thing (Greenleaf, 1977). Service and stewardship is not only an exercise in faith, but also one of responsibility and commitment.

Teachers as servant leaders may also stand alone, largely without the support of their colleagues and existing culture, as a saving remnant of those who care for students, families, administrators, institutions, and community interests who are determined to make their caring and service count—wherever they are involved and no matter whom they serve. This brings them, as serving individuals, constantly to a point where they examine the assumptions they live by; therefore, their service and leadership sustains trust (Greenleaf, 1977). By definition, trust suggests confidence and commitment to the responsibility of care for something or some individual without fear or misgiving. This confidence and commitment results in the creation of a cyclic process of care, trust, and continued service and stewardship.

The conundrum that teachers face is the fact that the call for education reform has been a recurring theme in the United States for more than two hundred years. It has continued to cause division among educators and communities, and currently stands at the pinnacle of our national debates that surround federal and state funding, No Child Left Behind legislation, and available Race to the Top federal funds under the current presidential administration. Since the beginning of the twentieth century, there have been more than thirty national reports and more than three hundred task forces that have been established by various states and the federal government to discover and explore how public schools can improve the quality of education (Giroux, 2004). These suggested reforms not only create a challenge for public educators, but also pose a threat to the teacher's significant role in public education and the ability to provide intellectual and moral leadership, as well as service, to today's youth and the next generation of community leaders.

The biggest problem with the current trend of more rigorous standards, accountability, and the testing and assessment movement, which includes the No Child Left Behind Act, is that it mistakes measuring schools for fixing them (Darling-Hammond, 2004). From the position of the federal policymakers, more tests means more accountability, and thus results in severe consequences for those that don't seem to perform and improve on an annual basis.

Unfortunately, these same policymakers don't really understand assessment and don't care to understand the struggles that many high-need schools, their teachers, their student populations, and their communities must overcome. The current trend is to focus only on test scores, and to downplay or ignore the significant role that teachers serve in preparing children to be active, critically thinking citizens. The focus remains on quantitative test measures and comparative trends, rather than the empowerment of teachers and educators and their abilities to use their intellect, judgment, and experience to improve the educational climate and the potential for all children to be successful and productive citizens.

As Giroux (2004) would suggest, the underlying theoretical assumption that guides federal and state mandates is that the behavior of teachers and the growth of their students need to be controlled, consistent, and predictable across different schools and different school populations. Unfortunately, these different schools, populations, and communities have vastly different needs. In effect, this approach works to de-skill teachers and remove them from the opportunity for service, reflection, and deliberation, as well as standardizing how teachers teach and how and what students will eventually learn. This assembly line model effectively produces students who are all the same, who think and act the same, and who will learn the same information, regardless of their individual backgrounds or personal strengths or struggles. This automatized trend eventually will not produce independent, creative, problem-solving, critical thinkers in our teaching force or among students in our classrooms. Neither will it produce service-oriented individuals who can understand the need to care for and serve others.

Simpson, Jackson, and Aycock (2005) offer suggestions for how schools should focus their energies using a modernized version of John Dewey's thoughts and ideas. These are suggestions that are worth repeating as teachers and administrators think about serving students, their parents, and their communities. As schools and teachers reform and reinvent themselves and their educational communities, they should:

- Build schools and classrooms that are genuine learning communities.
- Promote students' social and personal growth as educated citizens.
- Develop school curricula that value students' prior learning experiences.
- Understand each student outside of and in school environments.
- Study neighborhoods and cultures to align with the community and the school curriculum.
- Foster an artistic spirit in the school community.
- Create aesthetic learning experiences for all students.
- Cultivate students' understanding of facts, interpretations, and ideas as *tools* for thinking about and solving problems.
- Promote independent thinking and social responsibility among students and teachers.
- Expect and treat others with respect.
- Operate on the principle that each student and teacher is unique.
- Use their imaginations in thinking, learning, and teaching.
- Encourage courageous and experimental approaches to teaching and learning.

Understanding this great struggle to serve students, their families, our colleagues, the school administration, and the communities in which we work seems antithetical to the current focus on standards and testing. Serving is a benefit to the served and a blessing to those that serve. It may have nothing to do with meeting or understanding a curricular standard, and it may have nothing to do with testing students in an academic sense. It has a lot to do with understanding needs and filling a void where an emptiness exists.

The teacher as servant leader is a servant first, with the hope of leading others to service as a conscious choice. Although Greenleaf's text (1977) is targeted toward all those who serve and lead, particularly in the corporate world, his text should resonate and manifest itself with teachers and educators in the sense that as servants first, we should focus to make sure that other people's highest-priority needs are being served. Therefore, the supreme indicator of our success is, do those we serve grow as persons? Do they, while being served, become healthier, wiser, freer, more autonomous, and more likely themselves to become servants? And, as Greenleaf states, "what is the effect on the least privileged in society; will they benefit, or, at the least, not be further deprived?"

Servant leadership is about sacrifice and commitment to others. In schools, it is not just about serving, but also about encouraging and supporting a learning community of multiple stakeholders that includes children, their families, our colleagues and administrators, and the immediate community. It requires us to perhaps work outside of our comfort zones for a while, or for as long as it takes to make a difference in the lives of others. As teachers, we want our students to be deep, proficient, critical thinkers and learners. We also want them to become good people and, eventually, effective and caring community citizens.

By helping and encouraging our students and those in the educational community to see good examples of others who care, who are committed, and who are willing to serve, we ultimately impact the larger community and future generations of learners and servants. Teachers who are servant leaders have the unique ability to impact the future and to remain a permanent influence on those they serve. What greater results could teachers possibly desire?

References

Acosta, D., J. Keith, and D. Patin (1997). Home visits: Shortening the path between home and school. *Schools in the Middle, 7* (1), 24–25.

Adler, M. J. (1982). *The Paidea Proposal: An educational manifesto.* New York: Collier.

Angus, L. (1996). Cultural dynamics and organizational analysis: Leadership administration and the management of meaning in schools. In *International handbook of educational leadership and administration.* Leithwood, K., J. Chapman, D. Cirsib, P. Hallinger, and A. Hart (eds.). Boston: Kluwer, 967–996.

Appleton, N. (1983). *Cultural pluralism in education: Theoretical foundations.* New York: Longman.

Aronowitz, S., and H. A. Giroux (1985). *Education under siege.* South Hadley, MA: Bergin and Garvey.

Ayers, W. (2004). The standards fraud. In *Educational foundations: An anthology of critical readings.* Canestrari, A., and B. Marlowe (eds.). Thousand Oaks, CA: Sage Publications.

Banks, J. A. (1997). *Teaching strategies for ethnic studies.* Boston: Allyn & Bacon.

Banks, J. A., and C. A. M. Banks (eds.) (1995). *Handbook of research on multicultural education.* New York: Macmillan.

Baptiste, H. P. (1999). The multicultural environment of schools: Implications to leaders. In *The principal as leader.* Hughes, L. W. Upper Saddle River, NJ: Prentice Hall, 105–127.

Baptiste, H. P., and K. Hughes (1993, September). *Education in a multicultural society.* Paper presented at the Fourth International School Year 2020 Conference, Bogensee, Germany.

Baptiste, H. P., Jr., and M. L. Baptiste (eds.) (1980). *Multicultural teacher education: Preparing educators to provide educational equity* (Vol. 1). Washington, DC: American Association of Colleges for Teacher Education.

Barth, R. (2004). *Learning by heart*. San Francisco: Jossey-Bass Publishers.

Batcher, E. (1981). *Emotion in the classroom: A study of children's experience*. New York: Praeger.

Bennett, C. (1995). *Comprehensive multicultural education: Theory and practice*. Boston: Allyn & Bacon.

Bickman, M. (1999). Thoreau and the tradition of the active mind. In *Uncommon learning: Henry David Thoreau on education*. The Thoreau Society. New York: Houghton Mifflin Company, xix.

Blank, R. K. (1987). The role of the principal as leader: An analysis of variation in leadership of urban high schools. *Journal of Educational Research, 81*, 69–79.

Block, P. (1993). *Stewardship*. San Francisco: Berrett-Koehler Publishers.

Bolman, L., and T. Deal (2004). *Reframing organizations: Artistry, choice, and leadership*. San Francisco: Jossey-Bass Publishers.

Bomer, R., L. Dworin, L. May, and P. Semingson (2008). Miseducating teachers about the poor: A critical analysis of Ruby Payne's claims about poverty. *Teachers College Record, 110*, 34–42.

Boyer, E. (1995). *The basic school: A community for learning*. Princeton, NJ: The Carnegie Foundation for the Advancement of Teaching.

Brant, R. (1992). On building learning communities: A conversation with Hank Levin. *Educational Leadership, 50* (1), 19–23.

Bridgeland, W. M., and E. A. Duane (1986). The leadership of principals: Coping with turbulence. *Education, 107*, 212–219.

Bruner, J. (1990). *Acts of meaning*. Cambridge, MA: Harvard University Press.

Burns, J. M. (1978). *Leadership*. New York: Harper & Row.

Carr, A. A. (1997). *The participation "race": Kentucky's site-based decision teams*. Paper presented at the annual meeting of the American Educational Research Association, Chicago.

Casanova, U. (1987). Ethnic and cultural differences. In *Educator's handbook: A research perspective*. Richardson-Koehler (ed.). White Plains, NY: Longman.

Chira, S. (1993, June 23). What do teachers want most? Help from parents. *New York Times*, 17.

Chusmire, L. H., and C. S. Koberg (1987). Organizational culture relationships with creativity and other job-related variables. *Journal of Business Research, 15*, 397–409.

Comillion, M. M. (1991). 3.5 plus. *Strange new world, 1* (4), 14–24.

Covington, J. (2007). Leading successful, sustainable change. *Course and direction: The path to strategic success.* Chesapeake Consulting, Inc. Retrieved June 11, 2007, from http://www.strategyletter.com.

Crago, M. B., B. Annahatak, and L. Ningiuruvik (1993). Changing patterns of language socialization in Inuit homes. *Anthropology and Education Quarterly, 24,* 205–223.

Csikszentmihalyi, M. (1990). *Flow.* New York: Harper Perennial.

Cubberly, E. (1909). *Changing conceptions of education.* New York: Riverside Educational Mimeographs.

Darling-Hammond, L. (2004). From "separate but equal" to "no child left behind": The collision of new standards and old inequalities. In *Many children left behind.* Meier, D., and G. Wood (eds.). Boston: Beacon Press.

Davies, D. (1993). Benefits and barriers to parent involvement: From Portugal to Boston to Liverpool. In *Families and schools in a pluralistic society.* Chavkin, N. (ed.). Albany: State University of New York Press, 205–216.

Davis, G. A. (1995). *How to involve parents in a multicultural school.* Alexandria, VA: The Association for Supervision and Curriculum Development.

Davis, G. A., and M. A. Thomas (1989). *Effective schools and effective teachers.* Needham Heights, MA: Allyn & Bacon.

Deci, E. L. (1971). Effects of externally mediated rewards on intrinsic motivation. *Journal of Personality and Social Psychology, 18,* 105–15.

Delgado-Gaitan, C. (1994). Socializing young children in Mexican-American families: An intergenerational perspective. In *Cross-cultural roots of minority child development.* Greenfield, P. M., and R. R. Cocking (eds.). Mahwah, NJ: Erlbaum.

Dewey, J. (1882–1898). *The early works of John Dewey, 1882–1898.* Southern Illinois University Press.

Dewey, J. (1899–1924). *The middle works of John Dewey, 1899–1924.* Southern Illinois University Press.

Dewey, J. (1916). *Democracy and education.* New York: Macmillan.

Dewey, J. (1925–1953). *The later works of John Dewey.* Southern Illinois University Press.

Digiulio, R. (2010). Psst . . . It ain't about the tests: It's still about great teaching. In *Educational Foundations: An anthology of critical readings.* 2nd ed. Canestrari and Marlowe (eds.). Thousand Oaks, CA: Sage Publications.

Dolan, W. P. (1994). *Restructuring our schools: A primer on systematic change.* Kansas City: Systems and Organizations.

Donnell, K. (2010). Beyond the deficit paradigm: An ecological orientation to thriving urban schools. In *Education foundations: An anthology of critical readings.* Canestrari, A., and B. Marlowe (eds.). Thousand Oaks, CA: Sage Publications, 161–167.

Duran, B. J., and R. E. Weffer (1992). Immigrants' aspirations, high school process, and academic outcomes. *American Educational Research Journal, 29,* 163–181.

Dweck, C. S. (1986). A social-cognitive approach to motivation and personality. In *Psychological Review, 95,* 256–73.

Eberly, D. (1995). Building the habit of character. In *The content of America's character.* Eberly, D. (ed.). Lanham, MD: Madison Books, 25–44.

Eccles, J., and R. Harold (1996). Family involvement in children's and adolescents' schooling. In *Family-school links: How do they affect educational outcomes?* Booth, A., and J. Dunn (eds.). Mahwah, NJ: Erlbaum, 3–24.

Emerson, R. W. (1982). *Emerson in his journals.* Porte, J. (ed.). Cambridge: Harvard University Press.

Emerson, R. W. (1983). *Essays and journals.* Joel Porte (ed.). New York: Library of America.

Epstein, J. L. (1996). Perspectives and previews on research and policy for school, family, and community partnerships. In *Family-school links: How do they affect educational outcomes?* Booth, A., and J. Dunn (eds.). Mahwah, NJ: Erlbaum.

Epstein, J. L. (2001). *School, family, and community partnerships.* Boulder, CO: Westview Press.

Epstein J. L. (2005). Results of the partnership schools—CRS Model for student achievement. *Elementary School Journal, 106,* 151–170.

Epstein, J. L. (2007a). Family and community involvement. In *American high school: An encyclopedia.* Borman, K., S. Cahill, and B. Cotner (eds.). Westport, CT: Greenwood Publishing.

Epstein, J. L. (2007b). Homework. In *American High School: An encyclopedia.* Borman, K., S. Cahill, and B. Cotner (eds.). Westport, CT: Greenwood Publishing.

Epstein, J. L., and S. B. Sheldon (2006). Moving forward: Ideas for research on school, family, and community partnerships. In *Sage handbook for research in education.* Conrad, C. F., and R. Serlin (eds.). Thousand Oaks, CA: Sage Publications.

Fraser, B., G. Anderson, and H. Walberg (1982). *Assessment of learning environments: Manual for learning environment inventory (LEI) and my class inventory (MCI).* 3rd ed. Perth: Western Australia Institute of Technology.

Freire, P. (1970). *Pedagogy of the oppressed.* Continuum International Publishing Group.

French, J., and B. Raven (1959). The bases of social power. In *Studies in social power.* Cartwright, D. (ed.). Ann Arbor, MI: Center for Social Research, 150–165.

Friend, M. (2006). *Special education* (IDEA 204, Updated.). Boston: Allyn & Bacon.

Fullan, M. (2005). *Leadership and sustainability.* Thousand Oaks, CA: Corwin Press.

Garcia, E. E. (1992). "Hispanic" children: Theoretical, empirical, and related policy issues. *Educational Psychology Review, 4,* 69–93.

Garcia, E. E. (1994). *Understanding and meeting the challenge of student cultural diversity*. Boston: Houghton Mifflin.

Garcia, E. E. (1995). Educating Mexican American students: Past treatment and recent developments in theory, research, policy, and practice. In *Handbook of research on multicultural education*. Banks, J. A., and C. A. M. Banks (eds.). New York: Macmillan.

Gardner, H. (1995). *Leading minds: An anatomy of leadership*. New York: Harper Collins Publishing.

Garrison, L. (1989). Programming for the gifted American Indian student. In *Critical issues in gifted education: Vol. 2. Defensible programs for cultural and ethnic minorities*. Maker, C. J., and S. W. Schiever (eds.). Austin, TX: Pro-Ed.

Gilliland, H. (1988). Discovering and emphasizing the positive aspects of the culture. In *Teaching the Native American*. Gilliland, H., and J. Reyhner (eds.). Dubuque, IA: Kendall/Hunt.

Ginott, H. (1972). *Teacher & child*. New York: Macmillan.

Giroux, H. (2004). Teachers as transformative intellectuals. In *Educational foundations: An anthology of critical readings*. Canestrari, A. S, and B. A. Marlowe (eds.). Thousand Oaks, CA: Sage Publications.

Goldenburg, C., R. Gallimore, L. Reese, and H. Garnier (2001). Cause or effect? A longitudinal study of immigrant Latino parents' aspirations and expectations, and their children's school performance. *American Educational Research Journal, 38*, 547–582.

Goldstein, S. (1995). *Understanding and managing children's classroom behavior*. New York: Wiley.

Gollnick, D. M., and P. C. Chinn (2002). *Multicultural education in a pluralistic society*. 6th ed. Upper Saddle River, NJ: Merrill/Prentice Hall.

Gorski, P. (2006). Savage unrealities. *Rethinking Schools, 21* (2), 16–19.

Gorton, R., and G. Schneider (1991). *School-based leadership: Challenges and opportunities*. Dubuque, IA: Wm. C. Brown.

Gouldner, A. W. (1950). *Studies in leadership*. New York: Harper Brothers Publishing.

Grant, C. A., and M. L. Gomez (2001). *Campus and classroom: Making schooling multicultural*. 2nd ed. Upper Saddle River, NJ: Merrill/Prentice Hall.

Greenleaf, R. K. (1977). *Servant leadership*. New York: Paulist Press.

Gutierrez, K. D., and B. Rogoff (2003). Cultural ways of learning: Individual traits or repertoires of practice. *Educational Researcher, 32* (5), 19–25.

Hallahan, D. P., and J. M. Kauffman (2006). *Exceptional learners*. 10th ed. Boston: Allyn & Bacon.

Hargreaves, A. (2005, Winter). Sustainable leadership. *Independent School, 64* (2). Retrieved June 11, 2007, from http://library.genesee.edu:2061.

Harris, C. R. (1991). Identifying and serving the gifted new immigrant. *Teaching Exceptional Children, 23* (4), 26–30.

Harry, B., and J. Klinger (2007). Discarding the deficit model. *Educational Leadership, 64* (5), 16–21.

Heath, S. B. (1980). Questioning at home and at school: A comparative study. In *The ethnography of schooling: Educational anthropology in action.* Spindler, G. (ed.). New York: Holt, Rinehart & Winston.

Heath, S. B. (1989). Oral and literate traditions among black Americans living in poverty. *American Psychologist, 44,* 367–373.

Hill, N. E., and S. A. Craft (2003). Parent-school involvement and school performance: Mediated pathways among socioeconomically comparable African American and Euro-American families. *Journal of Educational Psychology, 95,* 74–83.

Hodgekinson, H. (1985). *All one system.* Washington, DC: The Institute for Educational Leadership.

Hodgekinson, H. (1988). Lecture at the University of Oklahoma National Conference on Race and Ethnic Relations in Higher Education, Norman, OK.

Hoerr, T. R. (2005). *The art of school leadership.* Alexandria, VA: The Association for Supervision and Curriculum Development.

Hoover, L., and J. Kindsvatter (1997). *Democratic discipline: Foundation and practice.* Upper Saddle River, NJ: Prentice Hall.

Hoover-Dempsey, K. V., and H. M. Sandler (1997). Why do parents become involved in their children's education? *Review of Educational Research, 67,* 3–42.

Hord, S. M., and W. A. Sommers (2008). *Leading professional learning communities: Voices from research and practice.* Thousand Oaks, CA: Corwin Press.

Hughes, L. W. (1999). *The principal as leader.* Upper Saddle River, NJ: Merrill/ Prentice Hall.

Hughes, L. W., and G. C. Ubben (1994). *The elementary principal's handbook: A guide to effective action.* Needham Heights, MA: Allyn & Bacon.

Igoa, C. (1995). The inner world of the immigrant child. Mahwah, NJ: Erlbaum.

Irujo, S. (1988). An introduction to intercultural differences and similarities in nonverbal communication. In *Toward multiculturalism: A reader in multicultural education.* Wurzel, J. S. (ed.). Yarmouth, ME: Intercultural Press.

Jackson, J. (1988). Common ground speech to the 1988 Democratic Convention, Atlanta.

Jensen, E. (2009). *Teaching with poverty in mind.* Alexandria, VA: The Association for Supervision and Curriculum Development.

Johnson, W., and A. Packard (1987). *Workplace 2000.* Indianapolis: Hudson Institute.

Kallen, H. (1956). *Cultural pluralism and the American ideal.* Philadelphia: University of Philadelphia Press.

Keedy, J. L. (1991). *School improvement practices of successful high school principals.* West Carrollton, GA: The West Georgia Regional Center for Teacher Education.

Killion, J., and P. Roy (2009). *Becoming a learning school.* Oxford, OH: National Staff Development Council.

Kirschenbaum, J. R. (1989). Identification of the gifted and talented American Indian student. In *Critical issues in gifted education: Vol. 2. Defensible programs for cultural and ethnic minorities.* Maker, C. J., and S. W. Schiever (eds.). Austin, TX: Pro-Ed.

Kohn, A. (1993, September). Choices for children: Why and how to let students decide. *Phi Delta Kappan,* 8–20.

Kohn, A. (1993). *Punished by rewards.* Boston: Houghton Mifflin.

Kohn, A. (1994). Grading: The issue is not how but why? *Educational Leadership.*

Kohn, A. (1999). Foreword in *Uncommon learning: Henry David Thoreau on education.* New York: Houghton Mifflin.

Kohn, A. (1999a). Developing a critical voice: A conversation with Alfie Kohn. In *Educational foundations: An anthology of critical readings.* Canestrari, A.S., and B. A. Marlowe (eds). Thousand Oaks, CA: Sage Publications.

Kohn, A. (1999b). *The schools our children deserve: Moving beyond traditional classrooms and "tougher standards."* Boston: Houghton Mifflin.

Kohn, A. (2004a). NCLB and the effort to privatize public education. In *Many children left behind.* Meier, D., and G. Wood (eds.). Boston: Beacon Press.

Kohn, A. (2004b). *What does it mean to be well educated?* Boston: Beacon Press.

Kouzes, J., and B. Posner (2003). *Credibility: How leaders gain and lose it, why people demand it.* San Francisco: Wiley & Sons.

Kozol, J. (1991). *Savage inequalities.* New York: Crown Publishers Inc.

Kraines, S. H. (1947). *Managing your mind.* New York: The Macmillian Company.

Krug, M. (1976). *The melting of the ethnics: Education of the immigrants, 1880–1914.* Bloomington, IN: Phi Delta Kappa Educational Foundation.

Lee, C. D., and D. T. Slaughter-Defoe (1995). Historical and sociocultural influences on African and American education. In *Handbook of research on multicultural education.* Banks, J. A., and C. A. M. Banks (eds.). New York: Macmillan.

Lee, V., A. Bryk, and J. Smith (1993). The organization of effective secondary schools. In *Review of Research in Education, 19,* 171–268. Darling-Hammond, L. (ed.).

Leithwood, K. (1990). The principal's role in teacher development. In *Changing school culture through staff development.* Joyce, B. (ed.). Alexandria, VA: The Association for Supervision and Curriculum Development, 71–90.

Lepper, M. R. (1973). Extrinsic rewards and intrinsic motivation. In *Teacher and student perceptions: Implications for learning.* Levin, J., and M. Wang (eds.). Hillsdale, NJ: Erlbaum.

Levin, D. U., and L. W. Lezotte (1995). Effective schools research. In *Handbook of research on multicultural education.* Banks, J. A., and C. A. M. Banks (eds.). New York: Macmillan.

Little, J. W. (2005). *On common ground: The power of professional learning communities.* Dufour, R., R. Eaker, and R. Dufour (eds). Bloomington, IN: Solution Tree.

Lomawaima, K. T. (1995). Educating Native Americans. In *Handbook of research on multicultural education.* Banks, J. A., and C. A. M. Banks (eds.). New York: Macmillan.

Losey, K. M. (1995). Mexican American students and classroom interaction: An overview and critique. *Review of Educational Research, 65,* 283–318.

Mackenzie, M. L. (2007, April/May). Leadership in the information age: A culture of continual change. *Bulletin.* Silver Spring, MD: American Society for Information Science and Technology. Retrieved September 23, 2007, from http://www.asis.org/Bulletin/Apr-07/mackenzie.html.

Manning, M. L., and L. G. Baruth (1996). *Multicultural education of children and adolescents.* Boston: Allyn & Bacon.

Mattingly, D. J., R. Prislin, T. L. McKenzie, J. L. Rodrigues, and B. Kayzar (2002). Evaluating evaluations: The case of parent involvement programs. *Review of Educational Research, 72,* 549–576.

McAlpine, L. (1992). Language, literacy, and education: Case studies of Cree, Inuit, and Mohawk communities. *Canadian Children, 17* (1), 17–30.

McCall, A. (1995). The bureaucratic restraints to caring in schools. In *Women leading education.* Dunlap, D., and P. Schmuck (eds.). Albany: State University of New York Press, 180–196.

McKeon, D. (1994). When meeting "common" standards is uncommonly difficult. *Educational Leadership, 51* (8), 45–49.

McLaren, P. L., and L. Lankshear (1993). Critical literacy and the postmodern turn. In *Critical literacy: Politics, praxis and the postmodern.* L. Lankshear & P. L. McLaren (eds.). Albany: State University of New York Press.

McMillan, D., and D. Chavis (1986). Sense of community: A definition and theory. *Journal of Community Psychology, 14,* 6–23.

Mehan, H. (1979). *Social organization in the classroom.* Cambridge, MA: Harvard University Press.

Meier, D. (2004). NCLB and democracy. In *Many children left behind.* Meier, D., and G. Wood (eds.). Boston: Beacon Press.

Meier, D. (2010). Resistance and courage. In *Educational foundations: An anthology of critical readings.* 2nd ed. Canestrari, A. S., and B. A. Marlowe (eds.). Thousand Oaks, CA: Sage Publications.

Menyuk, P., and D. Menyuk (1988). Communicative competence: A historical and cultural perspective. In *Toward multiculturalism: A reader in multicultural education.* Wurzel, J. S. (ed.). Yarmouth, ME: Intercultural Press.

Miller, L. S. (1995). *An American imperative: Accelerating minority educational advancement*. New Haven, CT: Yale University Press.

Minami, M., and A. McCabe (1996). Compressed expressions of experience: Some Asian American traditions. In *Chameleon readers: Some problems cultural differences in narrative structure pose for multicultural literacy programs*. McCabe, A. (ed.). New York: McGraw-Hill, 72–97.

Miranda, L. C. (1991). *Latino child poverty in the United States*. Washington, DC: Children's Defense Fund.

Moeller, A. J., and C. Reschke (1993). A second look at grading and classroom performance. *Modern Language Journal, 77*, 163–169.

Morrison, G. S. (2009). *Teaching in America*. Columbus, OH: Pearson Publishing.

Morrissey, M. (2000). *Professional learning communities: An ongoing exploration*. Austin, TX: Southwest Educational Development Laboratory.

Munroe, W. B. (1934). *Personality in politics*. New York: The Macmillan Company.

National Association of Bilingual Education (1993). Census reports sharp increase in number of non-English speaking Americans. *NABE News, 16* (6), 1, 25.

National Center for Educational Statistics (1997). *School-family linkages* [unpublished manuscript]. Washington, DC: U.S. Department of Education.

NCSS Task Force on Ethnic Studies Curriculum Guidelines (1992). Curriculum guidelines for multicultural education. *Social Education, 56*, 274–294.

Neisser, U. (1976). *Cognition and reality: Principles and implications of cognitive psychology*. New York: Freeman Press.

Newman, J. W. (2006). *America's teachers*. Boston: Allyn & Bacon Publishing.

Newmann, F. M., and G. Wehlage (1995). *Successful school restructuring: A report to the public and educators*. Madison, WI: Center on Organizational and Restructuring of Schools.

Newmann, F. M., G. Wehlage, and S. Lamborn (1992). The significance and sources of student engagement. In *Student engagement and achievement in American secondary schools*. Newmann, F. (ed.). New York: Teachers College Press, 11–39.

Ng, J. C., and J. Rury (2006). Poverty and education: A critical analysis of the Ruby Payne phenomenon. *Teachers College Record* (July 2006). Retrieved from www.trecord.org, ID Number 12596.

Nicholls, J. C., and J. P. Hazzard (1993). *Education as adventure: Lessons from the second grade*. New York: Teachers College Press.

Nieto, S. (2003). *Affirming diversity: The sociopolitical context of multicultural education*. 3rd ed. Boston: Allyn & Bacon Publishing.

O'Hair, M. J., and S. J. Odell (1993). *Diversity and teaching: Teacher education yearbook I*. Fort Worth, TX: Harcourt, Brace & Jovanovich.

Ogbu, J. U. (1992). Understanding cultural diversity and learning. *Educational Researcher, 21* (8), 5–14, 24.

Ogbu, J. U. (1999). Beyond language: Ebonics, proper English, and identity in a Black-American speech community. *American Educational Research Journal, 36*, 147–184.

Ohanian, S. (1999). *One size fits few.* Portsmouth, NH: Heinemann Pub.

Ormrod, J. E. (2010). *Educational Psychology 7th edition.* Upper Saddle River, NJ: Merrill/Prentice Hall.

Osei-Kofi, N. (2005). Pathologizing the poor: A framework for understanding Ruby Payne's work. *Equity and Excellence in Education, 38*, 367–375.

Page, M. (2010). Speaking in a critical voice. In *Educational foundations: An anthology of critical readings.* 2nd ed. Canestrari, A. S., and B. A. Marlowe (eds.). Thousand Oaks, CA: Sage Publications.

Pawlas, G. E. (1995). *School-community relations.* Princeton, NH: Eye on Education.

Payne, R. K. (2001). *A framework for understanding poverty.* Highland, TX: Aha! Process, Inc.

Peterson, K., and R. Brietzke (1994). *Building collaborative cultures: Seeking ways to reshape urban schools.* Oak Brook, IL: North Central Regional Educational Laboratory. (ERIC Document Reproduction Service No. ED 378 386).

Piaget, J. (1952). *The child's conception of the world.* London: Routledge & Kegan Paul.

Popham, J. (1995). *Classroom assessment: What teachers need to know.* Needham Heights, MA: Allyn & Bacon.

Postman, N., and C. Weingartner (1969). *Teaching as a subversive activity.* Dell Publishing, Random House.

Ramsey, P. G. (1987). *Teaching and learning in a diverse world: Multicultural education for young children.* New York: Teachers College Press.

Raywid, M. (1993). Community: An alternative school accomplishment. In *Public schools that work.* Smith, G. (ed.). New York: Routledge, 23–44.

Razik, T. A., and A. D. Swanson (2010). *Fundamental concepts of educational leadership and management.* Boston: Pearson Publishing.

Reid, N. (1989). Contemporary Polynesian conceptions of giftedness. *Gifted Education International, 6*(1), 30–38.

Renchler, R. (1993). Poverty and learning. *ERIC Digest.* Number 83. Eugene, OR: ERIC Clearinghouse on Educational Management.

Rogers-Healey, D. (2003, March 8). *12 insights into leadership for women.* Australian Virtual Centre for Leadership for Women. Retrieved September 23, 2007, from http://www.leadershipforwomen.com.au/questionnaire/12insights1.htm.

Rogoff, B. (2003). *The cultural nature of human development.* Oxford: Oxford University Press.

Roosevelt, T. *Citizen in a Republic Speech.* Sorbonne, Paris, on April 23, 1910.

Rost, J. (1991). *Leadership for the twenty-first century,* New York: Praeger.

Rowe, M. B. (1987). Wait-time: Slowing down may be a way of speeding up. *American Educator, 11*, 38–43, 47.

Salend, S . J., and L. Taylor (1993). Working with families: A cross-cultural perspective. *Remedial and Special Education, 14* (5), 25–32, 39.

Sanders, W. (2003). *Value-added approaches to school accountability: Results and lessons from an evaluation.* Paper presented at the annual meeting of the American Educational Research Association, Chicago.

Santrock, J. (2008). *Adolescence.* 12th ed. New York: McGraw-Hill Publishing.

Sarason, S. B. (2004). *The culture of the school and the problem of change.* Boston: Allyn & Bacon.

Sarte, J. P. (1978). Existentialism. In *Readings in the philosophy of education.* Rich, J. M. (ed.). Belmont, CA: Wadsworth Publishing.

Sato, M., and T. J. Lensmire (2009). Poverty and Payne: Supporting teachers to work with children of poverty. *Phi Delta Kappan, 90* (5), 365–370.

Scotti, W. H. (1987). Analysis of organizational incongruity using teacher perception of the principal's leadership behavior. *Education, 108* (1), 27–33.

Sergiovanni, T. J. (1994). *Moral leadership: Getting to the heart of school improvement.* San Francisco: Jossey-Bass Publishers.

Seyfarth, J. T. (1999). *The principal: New leadership for new challenges.* Upper Saddle River, NJ: Merrill.

Seyfarth, J. T. (1999). *The principal: New leadership for new challenges.* Upper Saddle River, NJ: Prentice Hall.

Simpson, D. J., M. J. B. Jackson, and J. C. Aycock (2005). *John Dewey and the art of teaching: Toward reflective and imaginative practice.* Thousand Oaks, CA: Sage Publications.

Simpson, D. J., M. J. B. Jackson, and J. C. Aycock (2005). *John Dewey and the art of teaching.* Thousand Oaks, CA: Sage Publications.

Sizer, T. (2004). Preamble: A reminder of Americans. In *Many children left behind.* Meier, D., and G. Wood (eds.). Boston: Beacon Press.

Skinner, B. F. (1983). *A matter of consequence.* New York: Knopf.

Slonim, M. B. (1991). *Children, culture, ethnicity: Evaluating and understanding the impact.* New York: Garland.

Stephenson, F. S. (2001). *Extraordinary teachers: The essence of excellent teaching.* Kansas City: Andrews McMeel Publishing.

Stiggins, R. J. (2001). *Student-involved classroom assessment.* 3rd ed. Upper Saddle River, NJ: Merrill/Prentice Hall.

Stigler, J. W., and J. Hiebert, J. (1999). *The teaching gap.* New York: The Free Press.

Sue, D. W. (1990). Culture-specific strategies in counseling: A conceptual framework. *Professional Psychology: Research and Practice, 21*, 424–433.

Tead, O. (1935). *The art of leadership*. New York: McGraw-Hill Publishing.

Tharp, R. G. (1989). Psychological variables and constants: Effects on teaching and learning in schools. *American Psychologist, 44*, 349–359.

Thoreau Society (1999). *Uncommon learning: Henry David Thoreau on education*. Bickman, M. (ed.), xxvii.

Thoreau, H. D. (1971). *Walden*. Shanley, L. D. (ed.). Princeton: Princeton University Press.

Thorndike, E. L. (1940). *Human nature and the social order*. New York: The Macmillan Company.

Tichy, H. J. (1988). *Scientific writing: Effective writing for engineers, managers, scientists*. New York: John Wiley & Sons.

Timm, J. T. (1996). *Four perspectives in multicultural education*. Belmont, CA: Wadsworth.

Timm, P., and K. Borman (1997). The soup pot don't stretch that far no more: Intergenerational patterns of school leaving in an urban Appalachian neighborhood. In *Beyond black and white: New faces and voices in U.S. schools*. Sellter, M., and L. Weis (eds.). Albany, NY: State University of New York Press.

Torres-Guzman, M. E. (1998). Language, culture, and literacy in Puerto Rican communities. In *Sociocultural contexts of language and literacy*. Perez, B. (ed.). Mahwah, NJ: Erlbaum.

Traina, R. (1999, January 20). What makes a teacher good? *Education Week, 18* (19), 34.

Trawick-Smith, J. (2003). *Early childhood development: A multicultural perspective*. 3rd ed. Upper Saddle River, NJ: Merrill/Prentice Hall.

Tudge, J., D. Hogan, S. Lee, P. Tammeveski, M. Meltsas, N. Kulakova, I. Snezhkova, and S. Putnam (1999). Cultural heterogeneity: Parental values and beliefs and their preschoolers' activities in the United States, South Korea, Russia, and Estonia. In *Children's engagement in the world: Sociocultural perspectives*. Goncu, A. (ed.). Cambridge: Cambridge University Press, 62–96.

U.S. Bureau of the Census (1994). *Statistical abstract of the United States: 1994*. 114th ed. Washington, DC: Author.

U.S. Bureau of the Census (1999). *Statistical abstract of the United States: 1999*. 115th ed. Washington, DC: Author.

Ubben, G. C., and L. W. Hughes (1997). *The principal: Creative leadership for effective schools*. 3rd ed. Boston: Allyn & Bacon.

Valdes, G. (1996). *Con respecto: Bridging the distances between culturally diverse families and schools*. New York: Teachers College Press.

Vasquez, J. A. (1988). Contexts of learning for minority students. *Educational Forum, 6*, 243–253.

Vygotsky, L. (1978). *Mind in society*. Cambridge, MA: Harvard University Press.

Wagner, T. (2001, July). Leadership for learning. *Phi Delta Kappan, 82* (5), 378–383.

Wallace, G. (1996). Relating to teachers. In *School improvements: What can pupils tell us?* Ruddick, J., R. Chaplain, and G. Wallace (eds.). London: Fulton, 29–40.

Warren, A. R., and L. A. McCloskey (1993). Pragmatics: Language in social contexts. In *The development of language*. 3rd ed. Berko Gleason, J. (ed.). New York: Macmillan.

Weber, C. A., and M. E. Weber (1961). *Fundamentals of educational leadership*. New York: Exposition Press.

Weiner, B. (1979). A theory of motivation for some classroom experiences. *Journal of Educational Psychology, 71*, 3–25.

Wetlaufer, S. (2000, July). Who wants to manage a millionaire? *Harvard Business Review, 78* (4).

White, P. (1996). *Civic virtues and public schooling*. New York: Teachers College Press.

Whitman, W. (1856). *Leaves of Grass*. Self-published.

Wlodkowski, R. J., and M. B. Ginsberg (1995). *Diversity and motivation: Culturally responsive teaching*. San Francisco: Jossey-Bass.

Wood, G. (2004). NCLB's effects on classrooms and schools. In *Many children left behind*. Meier, D., and G. Wood (eds.). Boston: Beacon Press.

Yao, E. (1993). Strategies for working effectively with Asian immigrant parents. In *Families and schools in a pluralistic society*. Chavkin, N. (ed.). Albany, NY: State University of New York Press, 149–155.

Yeager, R. J. (1985). Introducing Edward L. Bernays, the "father of public relations." *Momentum, 12*, 28–29.

Yee, A. H. (1992). Asians as stereotypes and students: Misperceptions that persist. *Educational Psychology Review, 4*, 95–132.

Zill, N. (1996). Family change and student achievement: What we learned, what it means for schools. In *Family-school links: How do they affect educational outcomes?* Booth, A., and J. Dunn (eds.). Mahway, NJ: Erlbaum, 139–174.

Index

~

About the Author

Joe D. Nichols grew up in Oklahoma dodging tornadoes in the spring, enjoying the wheat harvest in the summer, and appreciating the wide-open spaces of the Midwest. He completed a bachelor's degree in math education at Southwestern Oklahoma State University in 1979. After graduation, he married Get, a first-grade teacher and his high school sweetheart, and taught middle school and high school mathematics in the Moore Public School System in Moore, Oklahoma, for fifteen years. Along the way, he completed his master's degree in school counseling and his Ph.D. in educational psychology, both from the University of Oklahoma. He currently is professor and chair of the Department of Educational Studies in the School of Education at Indiana University–Purdue University Fort Wayne in Indiana.

Breinigsville, PA USA
12 October 2010
247142BV00002B/1/P